CHRISTINA ROSSETTI

CHRISTINA ROSSETTI

Selected Poems

Edited by C. H. Sisson

Fyfield*Books*

First published in 1984 by
Carcanet Press Limited
208–212 Corn Exchange Buildings
Manchester M4 3BQ

British Library Cataloguing in Publication Data

Rossetti, Christina
  Selected poems.–(Fyfield books)
  I. Title   II. Sisson, C. H.
  821'.8   PR5237.A4

ISBN: 0 85635 533 X

The publisher acknowledges the financial assistance
of the Arts Council of Great Britain

Printed in England by SRP Ltd, Exeter

CONTENTS

7

INTRODUCTION

'CHRISTINA ROSSETTI seems to us to be the most valuable poet that the Victorian age produced.' So Ford Madox Ford, seventy or eighty years ago, when the shadows of the inflated great still stalked. Not only are Alfred Lord Tennyson and Robert Browning, Arnold and Swinburne and a range of other meditative and prophetic characters taken down a peg or two by Ford's dictum; in the essay in *The Critical Attitude* from which it is taken he is asserting that Christina Rossetti, more than any of the others, indicated the direction in which the poetry of the twentieth century was to move. This diagnosis, which must have seemed lunatic to many readers in 1911, has been confirmed by much that has happened since then and is hardly questionable in the 1980s. The simplicity and directness of her language, the intimate fall of her rhythms, make her immediately accessible in a way that the more over-sized figures are not.

Some hindrances to a proper estimate of Christina's work remain. Although in the best of her poems the social and religious background does not obtrude itself, it is something that anyone who reads her work in bulk must come to terms with, and that background is remote from our own. But to become acquainted with orientations different from our own, without being shocked by attitudes which are unfamiliar to us, is part of the benefit of reading the authors of times other than our own; it is also one of the reasons why literature is central to anything like a humane education, whatever other studies may be hawked as alternatives. With Christina—one cannot, even out of respect for a feminist passion for surnames, call her simply Rossetti, for she has to be distinguished from her more famous and cossetted brother, the poet and painter Dante Gabriel—there is a domestic background which restricted her freedom of movement in a manner then thought proper but now improper, and an absorption in a religious milieu which will seem strange to many besides those to whom Christianity itself has come to seem remote. Yet, as Ford says, Christina 'dealt hardly at all in ideas: nearly every one of her poems was an instance, was an illustration of an emotion'. And human emotions persist through all the changes of circumstance and ideology.

It was Christina's isolation—an isolation which persisted even in a circle which originally included Italian revolutionaries as well as such figures as Coventry Patmore, William Morris, Ruskin, Browning, Swinburne, Gosse and Hall Caine, to say nothing of the Pre-Raphaelite Brotherhood when it was a rising force— which enabled her to stand aside from so much of the ordinary nonsense of the age and to concentrate so intensely on the events of her own inner life and to speak of them with such purity of diction. While her gifted but arty brother and his friends were intent on amazing the world, 'up in the fireless top back bedroom on the corner of the cracked washstand'—this is Ford once again—'on the backs of old letters Christina sat writing'. This life of abnegation is horrifying, in terms of our current pre-possessions. One may speculate as to what she might have done if, as was at one time in prospect, she had gone to Scutari with Florence Nightingale. But this did not happen, and wider experience does not always mean deeper experience, nor would the excursion necessarily have led to a more probing alternative to 'The Charge of the Light Brigade'. The life Christina did in fact live enabled her to write the poems she did in fact write. That is all that concerns us and, given the quality of the poems, it is enough.

The place of Christina's birth was 38 Charlotte Street, Portland Place, London; the date, 1830. She was the youngest of four children, the relatively short annual production line starting in 1827 with Maria Francesca, who became a nun. Dante Gabriel came next and was followed by William Michael, whose career as a civil servant was for some time the mainstay of the family; he was a man of articles and reviews who edited among other things the posthumous collection of his sister's poems. The father of the four children was Gabriele Rossetti, born in 1783 in what was then the kingdom of Naples, the son of a blacksmith and locksmith; he became in turn an official operatic librettist and the custodian of ancient bronzes in the Naples museum. Gabriele came to London in 1824 as a refugee; following the break-up of Napoleon's Europe he had taken too much interest in politics for the Bourbon king of Naples. In April 1826 he married the daughter of Gaetano Polidori who had been secretary to the poet Alfieri and had come to England, after witnessing the fall of the Bastille, to teach Italian. His wife—Christina's maternal grandmother—was of a family so English that her father, so it is said, found it hard to understand why she had married a foreigner. In London Gabriele Rossetti, like his father-in-law, taught Italian for a living; he even held the distinguished, but then unremunerative, post of Professor of Italian at King's College, London. He published verse in his native language which was banned in Italy and won him some reputation there as a patriotic poet; also prose books in which he developed somewhat esoteric views about Dante and opposed, as William says, 'the papal system and its pretensions'. The family to which Christina belonged was thus what might be characterized as intellectual and not particularly well off, though well enough for plain living; and she was three-quarters Italian. The children were baptised and brought up in the Church of England, and it was in the world of Victorian Anglo-Catholicism that Maria and Christina lived out their religious lives. None the less, Italian influences were prominent in their early years. Since no one who has written on the subject was better placed than William Michael to give an account of the family at that time it is worth quoting what he has to say at some length.

'The children', he writes in the introduction to Christina's

Collected Poems (1904), 'were constantly with their parents; there was no separate nursery, and no rigid lines drawn between the big one and the little ones. Of English society there was extremely little—barely one or two families that we saw something of at moderate intervals; but of Italian society—in the sense of Italians who hunted up and haunted our father as an old acquaintance or as a celebrity—the stream was constant and copious. Singular personages these Italians (with occasionally some foreigner of a different nationality) were, in many instances; almost all of them eager after something—few or none eager to increase his income, to rise a grade in position, to set his children going in one of the approved grooves, to relax over the sporting columns of a newspaper. There were exiles, patriots, politicians, literary men, musicians, some of them of inferior standing; fleshy and good-natured Neapolitans, keen Tuscans, emphatic Romans. As we children were habituated from our earliest years to speaking Italian with our father, we were able to follow the speech of these 'natives'; and a conspirator or semi-brigand might well present himself, and open out on his topics of predilection, without our being told to leave the room. All this—even apart from our own chiefly Italian blood—made us, no doubt, not a little different from British children in habit of thought and standard of association.' On the other hand, the education of the girls was 'entirely undertaken' by their mother, who was half English and had been a governess in an English family.

There is an extraordinary document of Christina's young womanhood or perhaps one should say rather adolescence, for the tone of it is certainly adolescent although she was probably about eighteen when she wrote it. This is *Maude, A Story for Girls*, which was published in a limited edition by William Michael nearly half a century after it was written. The story takes us into a world which would certainly be strange to any girl of eighteen at the present time or at any time during the

12

present century. It is mawkish; it presents a virtually closed world of young ladies wrapped up in mutual friendship and in ordinary domestic exchanges. Christina's Maude is undoubtedly a self-portrait, and a highly critical one—but critical with standards of scrupulosity and it must be said religiosity for which, in 1897, the editor brother felt the need to make some smiling apology. The 'worst harm' this girl appears to have done, he says, 'is that, when she had written a good poem she felt it to be good'. It must be said that this is a conscientious caution of which more might with advantage be heard, in these days when verses less good than Maude's are often admired rather freely by their authors. Some of her other crimes are strictly religious, even ecclesiastical. She is guilty of preferring not to take communion when she supposes herself to be unworthy of it and of going to a church other than her parish church because the music is better. If these concerns seem extravagant they are at the opposite pole from the fault of assuming the rightness of one's actions whatever they may be—an infinitely commoner fault and one to which the irreligious are as much subject as anybody. Part of the pleasure in reading the story, for the present-day reader, will certainly be in what must seem the absurdity of the milieu and many of its preoccupations, but even at this age Christina is writing well. The style is lucid and agreeable and any present-day undergraduate who thinks he is entitled to scorn it should look to his own prose. The work is of course extremely immature and far from the point Christina reached in her later development. But with any poet the starting-point, social as well as literary, is worth finding out about, and as first-hand evidence of where Christina set out from *Maude* is worth the short time it takes to read.

There are one or two touches in the story which show us the young author with particular vividness. 'It was the amazement of everyone what could make her poetry so broken-hearted', but' "I sleep like a top," Maude put in drily.' Above all there is

13

the scene in which Maude copies out a melancholy sonnet she has written, 'having done which she yawned, leaned back in her chair, and wondered how she should fill up the time till dinner.' The sonnet—an extraordinary one for a girl of this age—is the one beginning, 'Yes, I too could face death and never shrink'. William Michael dates this poem 1850, and there is reason to think that it may be a little later than the original prose text. Christina was, in any case, quickly out of the world of girlish friendships delineated in *Maude* and into a love affair which marked her for life.

Dorothy Margaret Stuart who wrote the *English Men of Letters* volume on Christina ('*Men* of Letters' indeed!) seems reluctant to see James Collinson as a serious contender for her affections and supposes that her 'youth and inexperience' were such that her brothers' recommendation of this 'colourless, inoffensive person' was enough to make her 'imagine that she was in love when she was nothing of the kind'. Stuart's reasons for supposing such a thing of a girl who certainly knew her own mind and went her own way—however quiet a one it may have been—are entirely unconvincing; one is left with a suspicion that they include the fact that Collinson 'belonged to the superior tradespeople class' and that the family was provincial. However that may be, Stuart relies partly on her own rather foolish notions of the sort of poems Christina would have written during the courtship if she had really been in love; she also finds it hard to credit her subject's objection to Roman Catholicism. The outlines of the story are these: Christina was introduced to Collinson, a painter and one of the Pre-Raphaelite Brotherhood, by Dante Gabriel when she was not yet eighteen. Collinson had been brought up, like Christina, in the Church of England, but he had become a Roman Catholic. She declined his proposal; he became an Anglican again and she accepted him. Then he once more became a Roman Catholic and that finished him as far as Christina was concerned. 'A right-meaning man, of timorous

14

conscience' is how William Michael describes Collinson; one could be more unkind. There is no doubt that for Christina, to refuse her lover was a terrible act of renunciation—a 'staggering blow . . . from which she did not fully recover for years', her brother says. The fact that Collinson was 'an insignificant little man with a thick neck', somewhat lachrymose and a thorough mediocrity, has nothing to do with the matter for when was Love not blind?

There was a further offer of marriage later—in 1866, after an acquaintance of some six years—from a man called Charles Bagot Cayley, a suitor much preferred by Stuart as 'a gentleman and a scholar' as against the 'plebeian of very moderate intellectual attainments'. Here the objection was again a matter of conscience on Christina's part; Cayley was uncertain as to what, if anything, he did believe. There is no doubt that he would not have interfered with the religious education of his children in the way that Collinson would certainly have done. The exact nature of Christina's scruples cannot be known, indeed very little can be known about her specific reflections on these affairs, for she was extremely reticent. Certainly her general integrity and her honesty in the smallest matters were such that any sort of prevarication must have been matter for revulsion for her. But it has to be admitted that she was churchy as well as religious; her life was centred on ritual practices and obedience to the directions of the clergy to a degree which must have presented difficulties if she had been the centre of a family instead of merely a member of one, however helpful and careful of her duties in the latter connection. Moreover, although as a girl she was vivacious and looked like becoming an expansive and sociable woman, this did not happen, for whatever reason or combination of reasons, and she early developed a disposition to discount herself and her wishes to an extent which made renunciation an ordinary habit of mind. This certainly has a bearing on her behaviour with Collinson and Cayley. She had rather indifferent health from the age of fifteen, and indeed throughout her life a series of illnesses which left her in middle age with permanent cardiac troubles. All this must be taken account of by anyone who is inclined to attribute psychological morbidities to her. She was markedly polite in her manner and her conversation was simple and lively, even witty. But the best account of Christina—and in the end the only one that matters—is that to be elicited from her poems. Nothing could present her more vividly than the opening lines of 'L.E.L.'

> Downstairs I laugh, I sport and jest with all;
> But in my solitary room above
> I turn my face in silence to the wall;
> My heart is breaking for a little love.

Whatever the importance of her affairs with Collinson and Cayley, it must not be forgotten that Christina, brought up in a lively and varied family, had strong domestic affections and the web of her interests extended into worlds very different from that of her ritualistic circles where, however, she also had close friends, and bereavements and other troubles certainly weighed upon her in her outwardly uneventful life. She was very fond of her Polidori grandparents, to whom she owed her early and virtually only acquaintance with non-urban surroundings; they died in 1853. She was devoted to her mother, who survived until 1886. Her life, if quiet by the standards of the nineteenth century and intolerably so by the standards of the twentieth, was full of inner concerns.

It is these concerns which fill Christina's poetry. She began writing early and continued till shortly before her death in 1894. Her first verses, dictated when she was too young to write, are reputed to have been the lines, 'Cecilia never went to school/Without her gladiator.' Her first surviving written poem is eight lines for her mother's birthday, unremarkable enough but showing great competence for a child of twelve. After that date there were often verses, in English or Italian, and in 1847 there was a privately printed collection from a press run by grandfather Polidori with the help of a Sicilian compositor. If the poems are not such as would have enabled anyone to foresee her later work, they are certainly such that, looking back with her mature work in mind, one could recognize them as Christina's.

The first published volume came fifteen years later, in 1862. *Goblin Market and other poems*, the volume in question, contains some of her best work and the title poem was the first Pre-Raphaelite writing to catch public attention. Dante Gabriel's first book (with 'The Blessed Damozel') was not published till 1870 and Swinburne's *Atalanta in Calydon* only in 1865. So this unlikely young woman, who never spoke about her own poetry if she could help it, stole a march on those flamboyant professionals and became the spearhead of the new poetry of the final third of the century. 'Up Hill' and two other poems had appeared successively in *Macmillan's Magazine* in 1861 and it was Macmillans who became and remained Christina's publisher. The volume had a frontispiece in black-and-white by Dante Gabriel—a characteristic Rossetti drawing—and had some success, though apparently not only Mrs Gaskell but John Ruskin failed to appreciate the new phenomenon. The tone of 'Up Hill'— world-weary as the poetry of the end of the century was to be, but stoical and religious—must have had at once novelty and familiarity for the reader of 1862 and the simplicity of the language was such as to attract any who were unprejudiced enough not to know what the language of poetry should be like. 'Goblin Market' stands alone among Christina's own work as it does in the wider context of the century's poetry. 'It has', as David Wright says, 'a vitality and sensuousness allied to simplicity, clearness, and intellectual coherence, in notable contrast to the lushness of most of the poetry of the period.' 'Intellectual coherence' is not a quality which will readily have been attributed to the poem but Christina, though not much of a reader

17

of theological works, had so thoroughly absorbed the central doctrines of historical Christianity that she so to speak uses the system without a thought; the coherence of the system and her own personal integrity have as it were become one and the same thing. Of course the reader does not need to recognize the doctrine to enjoy the poem, and it is indeed the last thing that most readers will think of as they let themselves move into the strange images and rapid and eccentric rhythms of the tale. 'Goblin Market' has often passed as a poem for children. That it has done so is a tribute to its immediacy, which can take the breath of anyone with an ear and an eye for poetry, but the sexual undertones of the story of temptation and devotion are evident at once to an adult.

The next volume, published in 1866, also contained a long poem, 'The Prince's Progress'. The history of this poem is of interest. What became the last sixty lines of a poem of over five hundred were written on a single day in 1861, the rest four years later at the instance of Dante Gabriel. What had simply been a dirge with the authentic tone, as well as the verbal limpidity, of Christina's lyric manner became a narrative not without grace in the telling but patently allegorical and with none of the spontaneity which sustains 'Goblin Market'. The notion of planning and working out a poem was foreign to Christina and much more in Dante Gabriel's manner than her own. We know that she resisted some of her brother's suggestions—he would, for example, have had a *tournament* in it, in the best Victorian fashion. All the evidence we have about Christina's own method of composition is that her work was occasional and spontaneous; it came, in Keats's words, 'as easily as the leaves of a tree' and it is this which gives the best poems their naturalness and wholeness. The original dirge is properly her own sort of poetry as the narrative is not and it alone is included in this selection. Other poems from the 1866 volume include 'Memory', the first part of which clearly refers to Collinson and the second to Cayley; it contains some of Christina's most poignant and characteristic verses:

> I shut the door to face the naked truth,
>   I stood alone—I faced the truth alone.
> Stripped bare of self-regard or forms of ruth
>   Till first and last are shown.
>
> I took the perfect balances and weighed;
>   No shaking of my hand disturbed the poise;
> Weighed, found it wanting: not a word I said,
>   But silent made my choice.
>
> None know the choice I made; I make it still.
>   None know the choice I made and broke my heart,
> Breaking mine idol: I have braced my will
>   Once, chosen for once my part.
>
> I broke it at a blow, I laid it cold,
>   Crushed in my deep heart where it used to love.
> My heart dies inch by inch, the time grows old,
>   Grows old in which I grieve.

That is the essential Christina, at once controlled and passionate, unshakeable when her mind was made up. These characteristics may be recognized and admired even by contemporary readers whose conceptions are very different and to whom her conduct may seem bizarre as it is unfashionable. The style is the woman and nothing could be more unaffected than her use of language, designed not to impress or to amuse but to say what she has to say as simply as she can say it. This is the central core of all good writing. Christina's range may be small, but within that range she is complete master.

Sing-Song (1872) is a 'nursery rhyme book', not free from that touch of the factitious which all such productions have when compared with the residue of true nursery rhymes which

19

have travelled down the generations, but at their best showing something of Christina's ease and deftness.

> Who has seen the wind?
> Neither you nor I:
> But when the trees bow down their heads
> The wind is passing by.

The later work includes a large quantity—here only lightly represented—of specifically religious, one might say ecclesiastical work. *Called to be Saints* (1881)—containing only a few poems —is a compilation, largely biblical, designed to acquaint the reader with the occasions and meaning of the minor festivals of the Church; *Time Flies* (1885) is 'a reading diary' in which the poems are part of the texture of a course of devotional reading. Such volumes are certainly not for those who are approaching Christina's work for the first time. They are nearer to the spirit of Jeremy Taylor than to that of most of the religious writing of her own day and certainly remote from that of our own. I confess to finding them largely unreadable, but Christina's prose and verse in them are always direct and unassuming. It is not so much the width of her sympathies as the width of her experience that is in question; for one who had been among the artistic and free-thinking circles of her day she appears almost monastic. A trace of religiosity there may sometimes be, but there is nothing of the sentimental moralism which afflicted some Victorians; pretending is not in her line. Her religious reading was limited like that of many pious persons in earlier centuries; above all she knew her Bible inside out and her taste was formed above all by the superb and simple language of the Authorised Version. The gravity of her tone is free from all pretension.

The modern reader who is unfamiliar with these fields should by no means be put off. Those who approach Christina, from whatever point of view, simply as a poet—or even as what is now sometimes held, for reasons I am too old to understand,

20

to be that special thing, a Woman Poet—will find her one of a searing directness which puts several famous 'confessional' writers of our own time to shame. There is no showing off here, but in all her sobriety she is the most naked of poets.

COUPLET

'Come cheer up, my lads, 'tis to glory we steer'—
As the soldier remarked whose post lay in the rear.

MARY MAGDALENE

She came in deep repentance,
    And knelt down at His feet
Who can change the sorrow into joy,
    The bitter into sweet.

She had cast away her jewels
    And her rich attire,
And her breast was filled with a holy shame,
    And her heart with a holy fire.

Her tears were more precious
    Than her precious pearls—
Her tears that fell upon His feet
    As she wiped them with her curls.

Her youth and her beauty
    Were budding to their prime;
But she wept for the great transgression,
    The sin of other time.

Trembling betwixt hope and fear,
    She sought the King of Heaven,
Forsook the evil of her ways,
    Loved much, and was forgiven.

23

SPRING QUIET

Gone were but the Winter,
    Come were but the Spring,
I would go to a covert
    Where the birds sing;

Where in the whitethorn
    Singeth the thrush,
And a robin sings
    In the holly-bush.

Full of fresh scents
    Are the budding boughs
Arching high over
    A cool green house;

Full of sweet scents,
    And whispering air
Which sayeth softly:
    'We spread no snare;

'Here dwell in safety,
    Here dwell alone,
With a clear stream
    And a mossy stone.

'Here the sun shineth
    Most shadily;
Here is heard an echo
    Of the far sea,
        Though far off it be.'

SONG

When I am dead, my dearest,
    Sing no sad songs for me;
Plant thou no roses at my head,
    Nor shady cypress tree:
Be the green grass above me
    With showers and dewdrops wet:
And if thou wilt, remember,
    And if thou wilt, forget.

I shall not see the shadows,
    I shall not fear the rain;
I shall not hear the nightingale
    Sing on as if in pain:
And dreaming through the twilight
    That doth not rise nor set,
Haply I may remember,
    And haply may forget.

BITTER FOR SWEET

Summer is gone with all its roses,
    Its sun and perfumes and sweet flowers,
    Its warm air and refreshing showers:
    And even Autumn closes.

Yea, Autumn's chilly self is going,
    And Winter comes which is yet colder;
    Each day the hoar-frost waxes bolder,
    And the last buds cease blowing.

THREE STAGES

1.—*A Pause of Thought*

I looked for that which is not, nor can be,
  And hope deferred made my heart sick in truth:
  But years must pass before a hope of youth
    Is resigned utterly.

I watched and waited with a steadfast will:
  And though the object seemed to flee away
  That I so longed for, ever day by day
    I watched and waited still.

Sometimes I said: 'This thing shall be no more;
  My expectation wearies and shall cease;
  I will resign it now and be at peace':
    Yet never gave it o'er.

Sometimes I said: 'It is an empty name
  I long for; to a name why should I give
  The peace of all the days I have to live?'—
    Yet gave it all the same.

Alas thou foolish one! alike unfit
  For healthy joy and salutary pain:
  Thou knowest the chase useless, and again
    Turnest to follow it.

2.—*The End of the First Part*

My happy happy dream is finished with,
  My dream in which alone I lived so long.
My heart slept—woe is me, it wakeneth;
    Was weak—I thought it strong.

26

Oh weary wakening from a life-true dream!
　　Oh pleasant dream from which I wake in pain!
I rested all my trust on things that seem,
　　　And all my trust is vain.

I must pull down my palace that I built,
　　Dig up the pleasure-gardens of my soul;
Must change my laughter to sad tears for guilt,
　　　My freedom to control.

Now all the cherished secrets of my heart,
　　Now all my hidden hopes, are turned to sin.
Part of my life is dead, part sick, and part
　　　Is all on fire within.

The fruitless thought of what I might have been,
　　Haunting me ever, will not let me rest.
A cold North wind has withered all my green,
　　　My sun is in the West.

But, where my palace stood, with the same stone
　　I will uprear a shady hermitage:
And there my spirit shall keep house alone,
　　　Accomplishing its age.

There other garden-beds shall lie around,
　　Full of sweet-briar and incense-bearing thyme:
There will I sit, and listen for the sound
　　　Of the last lingering chime.

3.
I thought to deal the death-stroke at a blow:
To give all, once for all, but never more: —

Then sit to hear the low waves fret the shore,
　　Or watch the silent snow.

'Oh rest,' I thought, 'in silence and the dark:
Oh rest, if nothing else, from head to feet:
Though I may see no more the poppied wheat,
　　Or sunny soaring lark.

'These chimes are slow, but surely strike at last:
This sand is slow, but surely droppeth through:
And much there is to suffer, much to do,
　　Before the time be past.

'So will I labour, but will not rejoice:
Will do and bear, but will not hope again:
Gone dead alike to pulses of quick pain
　　And pleasure's counterpoise.'

I said so in my heart: and so I thought
My life would lapse, a tedious monotone:
I thought to shut myself and dwell alone
　　Unseeking and unsought.

But first I tired, and then my care grew slack,
Till my heart dreamed, and maybe wandered too:—
I felt the sunshine glow again, and knew
　　The swallow on its track:

All birds awoke to building in the leaves,
All buds awoke to fullness and sweet scent:
Ah too my heart woke unawares, intent
　　On fruitful harvest-sheaves.

Full pulse of life, that I had deemed was dead;
Full throb of youth, that I had deemed at rest.

Alas I cannot build myself a nest,
  I cannot crown my head

With royal purple blossoms for the feast,
Nor flush with laughter, nor exult in song:—
These joys may drift, as time now drifts along;
  And cease, as once they ceased.

I may pursue, and yet may not attain,
Athirst and panting all the days I live:
Or seem to hold, yet nerve myself to give
  What once I gave, again.

ONE CERTAINTY

Vanity of vanities, the Preacher saith,
 All things are vanity. The eye and ear
 Cannot be filled with what they see and hear.
Like early dew, or like the sudden breath
Of wind, or like the grass that withereth,
 Is man, tossed to and fro by hope and fear:
 So little joy hath he, so little cheer,
Till all things end in the long dust of death.
To-day is still the same as yesterday,
 To-morrow also even as one of them;
  And there is nothing new under the sun:
  Until the ancient race of Time be run,
 The old thorns shall grow out of the old stem,
And morning shall be cold and twilight grey.

TWO PURSUITS

A voice said, 'Follow, follow': and I rose
   And followed far into the dreamy night,
   Turning my back upon the pleasant light.
It led me where the bluest water flows,
And would not let me drink: where the corn grows
   I dared not pause, but went uncheered by sight
   Or touch: until at length in evil plight
It left me, wearied out with many woes.
Some time I sat as one bereft of sense:
   But soon another voice from very far
      Called, 'Follow, follow': and I rose again.
   Now on my night has dawned a blessed star:
      Kind steady hands my sinking steps sustain,
And will not leave me till I shall go hence.

A TESTIMONY

I said of laughter: it is vain.
   Of mirth I said: what profits it?
   Therefore I found a book, and writ
Therein how ease and also pain,
How health and sickness, every one
Is vanity beneath the sun.

Man walks in a vain shadow; he
   Disquieteth himself in vain.
   The things that were shall be again;
The rivers do not fill the sea,
But turn back to their secret source;
The winds too turn upon their course.

Our treasures moth and rust corrupt,
     Or thieves break through and steal, or they
     Make themselves wings and fly away.
One man made merry as he supped,
Nor guessed how when that night grew dim
His soul would be required of him.

We build our houses on the sand
     Comely withoutside and within;
     But when the winds and rains begin
To beat on them, they cannot stand:
They perish, quickly overthrown,
Loose from the very basement stone.

All things are vanity, I said:
     Yea vanity of vanities.
     The rich man dies; the poor man dies:
The worm feeds sweetly on the dead.
Whate'er thou lackest, keep this trust:
All in the end shall have but dust:

The one inheritance, which best
     And worst alike shall find and share:
     The wicked cease from troubling there,
And there the weary be at rest;
There all the wisdom of the wise
Is vanity of vanities.

Man flourishes as a green leaf,
     And as a leaf doth pass away;
     Or as a shade that cannot stay
And leaves no track, his course is brief:
Yet man doth hope and fear and plan
Till he is dead:—oh foolish man!

Our eyes cannot be satisfied
   With seeing, nor our ears be filled
   With hearing: yet we plant and build
And buy and make our borders wide;
We gather wealth, we gather care,
But know not who shall be our heir.

How should we hasten to arise
   So early, and so late take rest?
   Our labour is not good; our best
Hopes fade; our heart is stayed on lies.
Verily, we sow wind; and we
Shall reap the whirlwind, verily.

He who hath little shall not lack;
   He who hath plenty shall decay:
   Our fathers went; we pass away;
Our children follow on our track:
So generations fail, and so
They are renewed and come and go.

The earth is fattened with our dead;
   She swallows more and doth not cease:
   Therefore her wine and oil increase
And her sheaves are not numberèd;
Therefore her plants are green, and all
Her pleasant trees lusty and tall.

Therefore the maidens cease to sing,
   And the young men are very sad;
   Therefore the sowing is not glad,
And mournful is the harvesting.
Of high and low, of great and small,
Vanity is the lot of all.

A King dwelt in Jerusalem;
  He was the wisest man on earth;
  He had all riches from his birth,
And pleasures till he tired of them;
Then, having tested all things, he
Witnessed that all are vanity.

SONG

Oh roses for the flush of youth,
  And laurel for the perfect prime;
But pluck an ivy branch for me
  Grown old before my time.

Oh violets for the grave of youth,
  And bay for those dead in their prime;
Give me the withered leaves I chose
  Before in the old time.

AFTER DEATH

The curtains were half drawn, the floor was swept
  And strewn with rushes, rosemary and may
  Lay thick upon the bed on which I lay,
Where through the lattice ivy-shadows crept.
He leaned above me, thinking that I slept
  And could not hear him, but I heard him say,
  'Poor child, poor child': and as he turned away
Came a deep silence, and I knew he wept.
He did not touch the shroud, or raise the fold
  That hid my face, or take my hand in his,
    Or ruffle the smooth pillows for my head:

He did not love me living; but once dead
He pitied me; and very sweet it is
To know that he is warm though I am cold.

LOOKING FORWARD

Sleep, let me sleep, for I am sick of care;
    Sleep, let me sleep, for my pain wearies me.
Shut out the light; thicken the heavy air
With drowsy incense; let a distant stream
Of music lull me, languid as a dream,
    Soft as the whisper of a summer sea.

Pluck me no rose that groweth on a thorn,
    Nor myrtle white and cold as snow in June,
Fit for a virgin on her marriage morn:
But bring me poppies brimmed with sleepy death,
And ivy choking what it garlandeth,
    And primroses that open to the moon.

Listen, the music swells into a song,
    A simple song I loved in days of yore;
The echoes take it up and up along
The hills, and the wind blows it back again.—
Peace, peace, there is a memory in that strain
    Of happy days that shall return no more.

Oh peace! your music wakeneth old thought,
    But not old hope that made my life so sweet,
Only the longing that must end in nought.
Have patience with me, friends, a little while:
For soon, where you shall dance and sing and smile,
    My quickened dust may blossom at your feet.

34

Sweet thought that I may yet live and grow green,
    That leaves may yet spring from the withered root,
And buds and flowers and berries half unseen.
Then, if you haply muse upon the past,
Say this: Poor child, she has her wish at last;
    Barren through life, but in death bearing fruit.

REMEMBER

Remember me when I am gone away,
    Gone far away into the silent land;
    When you can no more hold me by the hand,
Nor I half turn to go yet turning stay.
Remember me when no more day by day
    You tell me of our future that you plann'd:
Only remember me; you understand
It will be late to counsel then or pray.
Yet if you should forget me for a while
    And afterwards remember, do not grieve:
    For if the darkness and corruption leave
    A vestige of the thoughts that once I had,
Better by far you should forget and smile
    Than that you should remember and be sad.

SEEKING REST

My mother said: 'The child is changed
    That used to be so still;
All the long day she sings and sings,
    And seems to think no ill;
She laughs as if some inward joy
    Her heart would overfill.'

My Sisters said: 'Now prythee tell
　　Thy secret unto us:
Let us rejoice with thee; for all
　　Is surely prosperous.
Thou art so merry: tell us, Sweet:
　　We had not used thee thus.'

My Mother says: 'What ails the child
　　Lately so blythe of cheer?
Art sick or sorry? Nay, it is
　　The winter of the year;
Wait till the Springtime comes again,
　　And the sweet flowers appear.'

My Sisters say: 'Come, sit with us,
　　That we may weep with thee:
Show us thy grief that we may grieve:
　　Yea haply, if we see
Thy sorrow, we may ease it; but
　　Shall share it certainly.'

How should I share my pain, who kept
　　My pleasure all my own?
My Spring will never come again;
　　My pretty flowers have blown
For the last time; I can but sit
　　And think and weep alone.

A PORTRAIT

1

She gave up beauty in her tender youth,
　　Gave all her hope and joy and pleasant ways;

She covered up her eyes lest they should gaze
On vanity, and chose the bitter truth.
Harsh towards herself, towards others full of ruth,
    Servant of servants, little known to praise,
    Long prayers and fasts trenched on her nights and days:
She schooled herself to sights and sounds uncouth
That with the poor and stricken she might make
    A home, until the least of all sufficed
Her wants; her own self learned she to forsake,
Counting all earthly gain but hurt and loss.
So with calm will she chose and bore the cross
    And hated all for love of Jesus Christ.

2

They knelt in silent anguish by her bed,
    And could not weep; but calmly there she lay.
    All pain had left her; and the last sun's ray
Shone through upon her, warming into red
The shady curtains. In her heart she said:
    'Heaven opens; I leave these and go away;
    The Bridegroom calls,—shall the Bride seek to stay?'
Then low upon her breast she bowed her head.
O lily flower, O gem of priceless worth,
    O dove with patient voice and patient eyes,
O fruitful vine amid the land of dearth,
    O maid replete with loving purities,
Thou bowedst down thy head with friends on earth
    To raise it with the saints in Paradise.

ENDURANCE

Yes, I too could face death and never shrink.
    But it is harder to bear hated life;

37

To strive with hands and knees weary of strife;
To drag the heavy chain whose every link
Galls to the bone; to stand upon the brink
   Of the deep grave, nor drowse tho' it be rife
   With sleep; to hold with steady hand the knife
Nor strike home:—this is courage, as I think.
Surely to suffer is more than to do.
   To do is quickly done: to suffer is
      Longer and fuller of heart-sicknesses.
   Each day's experience testifies of this.
Good deeds are many, but good lives are few:
      Thousands taste the full cup; who drains the lees?

WITHERING

Fade, tender lily,
   Fade, O crimson rose,
Fade every flower,
   Sweetest flower that blows.

Go, chilly autumn,
   Come, O winter cold;
Let the green stalks die away
   Into common mould.

Birth follows hard on death,
   Life on withering:
Hasten, we will come the sooner
   Back to pleasant spring.

TWILIGHT CALM

Oh pleasant eventide!
Clouds on the western side
Grow grey and greyer, hiding the warm sun:
The bees an birds, their happy labours done,
  Seek their close nests and bide.

Screened in the leafy wood
The stock-doves sit and brood:
The very squirrel leaps from bough to bough
But lazily; pauses; and settles now
  Where once he stored his food.

One by one the flowers close,
Lily and dewy rose
Shutting their tender petals from the moon:
The grasshoppers are still; but not so soon
  Are still the noisy crows.

The dormouse squats and eats
Choice little dainty bits
Beneath the spreading roots of a broad lime;
Nibbling his fill he stops from time to time
  And listens where he sits.

From far the lowings come
Of cattle driven home:
From farther still the wind brings fitfully
The vast continual murmur of the sea,
  Now loud, now almost dumb.

The gnats whirl in the air,
The evening gnats; and there

The owl opes broad his eyes and wings to sail
For prey; the bat wakes; and the shell-less snail
    Comes forth, clammy and bare.

    Hark! that's the nightingale,
    Telling the self-same tale
Her song told when this ancient earth was young:
So echoes answered when her song was sung
    In the first wooded vale.

    We call it love and pain,
    The passion of her strain;
And yet we little understand or know:
Why should it not be rather joy that so
    Throbs in each throbbing vein?

    In separate herds the deer
    Lie; here the bucks, and here
The does, and by its mother sleeps the fawn:
Through all the hours of night until the dawn
    They sleep, forgetting fear.

    The hare sleeps where it lies,
    With wary half-closed eyes;
The cock has ceased to crow, the hen to cluck:
Only the fox is out, some heedless duck
    Or chicken to surprise.

    Remote, each single star
    Comes out, till there they are
All shining brightly. How the dews fall damp!
While close at hand the glow-worm lights her lamp,
    Or twinkles from afar.

But evening now is done
As much as if the sun
Day-giving had arisen in the East—
For night has come; and the great calm has ceased,
The quiet sands have run.

TWO THOUGHTS OF DEATH

1

Her heart that loved me once is rottenness
    Now and corruption; and her life is dead
    That was to have been one with mine, she said.
The earth must lie with such a cruel stress
On eyes whereon the white lids used to press;
    Foul worms fill up her mouth so sweet and red;
    Foul worms are underneath her graceful head;
Yet these, being born of her from nothingness,
These worms are certainly flesh of her flesh.—
    How is it that the grass is rank and green
And the dew-dropping rose is brave and fresh
Above what was so sweeter far than they?
Even as her beauty hath passed quite away,
    Theirs too shall be as though it had not been.

2

So I said underneath the dusky trees:
    But, because still I loved her memory,
    I stooped to pluck a pale anemone,
And lo my hand lighted upon heartsease
Not fully blown: while with new life from these
    Fluttered a starry moth that rapidly
    Rose toward the sun: sunlighted flashed on me
Its wings that seemed to throb like heart-pulses.

Far far away it flew, far out of sight,—
　　From earth and flowers of earth it passed away
As though it flew straight up into the light.
　　Then my heart answered me: Thou fool, to say
　　That she is dead whose night is turned to day,
And no more shall her day turn back to night.

IS AND WAS

　She was whiter than the ermine
　　　That half-shadowed neck and hand,
　And her tresses were more golden
　　　Than their golden band;
　Snowy ostrich plumes she wore;
　Yet I almost loved her more
　In the simple time before.

　Then she plucked the stately lilies,
　Knowing not she was more fair,
　And she listened to the skylark
　　　In the morning air.
　Then, a kerchief all her crown,
　She looked for the acorns brown,
　Bent their bough, and shook them down.

　Then she thought of Christmas holly
　And the Maybloom in sweet May;
　Then she loved to pick the cherries
　　　And to turn the hay.
　She was humble then and meek,
　And the blush upon her cheek
　Told of much she could not speak.

　Now she is a noble lady
　With calm voice not overloud
　Very courteous in her action,

Yet you think her proud;
Much too haughty to affect;
Too indifferent to direct
Or be angry or suspect;
Doing all from self-respect.

THE THREE ENEMIES

The Flesh
'Sweet, thou art pale.'
                    'More pale to see,
Christ hung upon the cruel tree
And bore his Father's wrath for me.'

'Sweet, thou art sad.'
                    'Beneath a rod
More heavy, Christ for my sake trod
The winepress of the wrath of God.'

'Sweet, thou art weary.'
                    'Not so Christ;
Whose mighty love of me sufficed
For Strength, Salvation, Eucharist.'

'Sweet, thou art footsore.'
                    'If I bleed,
His feet have bled; yea in my need
His Heart once bled for mine indeed.'

The World
'Sweet, thou art young.'
                    'So He was young
Who for my sake in silence hung
Upon the Cross with Passion wrung.'

43

'Look, thou art fair.'
                        'He was more fair
Than men, Who deigned for me to wear
A visage marred beyond compare.'

'And thou hast riches.'
                        'Daily bread:
All else is His: Who, living, dead,
For me lacked where to lay His Head.'

'Life is sweet.'
                'It was not so
To Him, Whose Cup did overflow
With mine unutterable woe.'

The Devil

'Thou drinkest deep.'
                        'When Christ would sup
He drained the dregs from out my cup:
So how should I be lifted up?'

'Thou shalt win Glory.'
                        'In the skies,
Lord Jesus, cover up mine eyes
Lest they should look on vanities.'

'Thou shalt have knowledge.'
                                'Helpless dust!
In thee, O Lord, I put my trust:
Answer Thou for me, Wise and Just.'

'And Might.'—
                'Get thee behind me. Lord,
Who hast redeemed and not abhorred
My soul, oh keep it by Thy Word.'

THE SUMMER IS ENDED

Wreathe no more lilies in my hair,
For I am dying, Sister sweet:
Or, if you will for the last time
   Indeed, why make me fair
   Once for my winding sheet.

Pluck no more roses for my breast,
For I like them fade in my prime:
Or, if you will, why pluck them still,
   That they may share my rest
   Once more for the last time.

Weep not for me when I am gone,
Dear tender one, but hope and smile:
Or, if you cannot choose but weep,
   A little while weep on,
   Only a little while.

FROM THE ANTIQUE

The wind shall lull us yet,
   The flowers shall spring above us:
And those who hate forget,
   And those forget who love us.

The pulse of hope shall cease,
   Of joy and of regretting:
We twain shall sleep in peace,
   Forgotten and forgetting.

For us no sun shall rise,
    Nor wind rejoice, nor river,
Where we with fast-closed eyes
    Shall sleep and sleep for ever.

FOR ROSALINE'S ALBUM

Do you hear the low winds singing,
    The streams singing on their bed?—
Very distant bells are ringing
    In a chapel for the dead:—
    Death-pale better than life-red.

Mother, come to me in rest,
    And bring little May to see.
Shall I bid no other guest?
Seven slow nights have passed away
Over my forgotten clay:
    None must come save you and she.

NEXT OF KIN

The shadows gather round me, while you are in the sun:
  My day is almost ended, but yours is just begun:
The winds are singing to us both and the streams are singing still,
  And they fill your heart with music, but mine they cannot fill.

Your home is built in sunlight, mine in another day:
Your home is close at hand, sweet friend, but mine is far away:
  Your bark is in the haven where you fain would be:
I must launch out into the deep, across the unknown sea.

You, white as dove or lily or spirit of the light:
I, stained and cold and glad to hide in the cold dark night:
  You, joy to many a loving heart and light to many eyes:
I, lonely in the knowledge earth is full of vanities.

Yet when your day is over, as mine is nearly done,
  And when your race is finished, as mine is almost run,
You, like me, shall cross your hands and bow your graceful head:
Yea, we twain shall sleep together in an equal bed.

A PAUSE

They made the chamber sweet with flowers and leaves,
  And the bed sweet with flowers on which I lay;
  While my soul, love-bound, loitered on its way.
I did not hear the birds about the eaves,
Nor hear the reapers talk among the sheaves:
  Only my soul kept watch from day to day,
  My thirsty soul kept watch for one away:—
Perhaps he loves, I thought, remembers, grieves.
At length there came the step upon the stair,
  Upon the lock the old familiar hand:
Then first my spirit seemed to scent the air
  Of Paradise; then first the tardy sand
Of time ran golden; and I felt my hair
  Put on a glory, and my soul expand.

HOLY INNOCENTS

Sleep, little Baby, sleep;
  The holy Angels love thee,
And guard thy bed, and keep

A blessed watch above thee.
No spirit can come near
   Nor evil beast to harm thee:
Sleep, Sweet, devoid of fear
   Where nothing need alarm thee.

The Love which doth not sleep,
   The eternal Arms around thee:
The shepherd of the sheep
   In perfect love hath found thee.
Sleep through the holy night,
   Christ-kept from snare and sorrow,
Until thou wake to light
   And love and warmth to-morrow.

A WISH

I wish I were a little bird
   That out of sight doth soar;
I wish I were a song once heard
   But often pondered o'er,
Or shadow of a lily stirred
   By wind upon the floor,
Or echo of a loving word
   Worth all that went before,
Or memory of a hope deferred
   That springs again no more.

SEASONS

In Springtime when the leaves are young,
Clear dewdrops gleam like jewels, hung
On boughs the fair birds roost among.

When Summer comes with sweet unrest,
Birds weary of their mother's breast,
And look abroad and leave the nest.

In Autumn ere the waters freeze,
The swallows fly across the seas:—
If we could fly away with these!

In Winter when the birds are gone,
The sun himself looks starved and wan,
And starved the snow he shines upon.

BALLAD

'Soft white lamb in the daisy meadow,
  Come hither and play with me,
For I am lonesome and I am tired
  Underneath the apple tree.'

'There's your husband if you are lonesome, lady,
  And your bed if you want for rest:
  And your baby for a playfellow
  With a soft hand for your breast.'

'Fair white dove in the sunshine,
  Perched on the ashen bough,
Come and perch by me and coo to me
  While the buds are blowing now.

'I must keep my nestlings warm, lady,
  Underneath my downy breast:
There's your baby to coo and crow to you
  While I brood upon my nest.'

49

'Faint white rose, come lie on my heart,
    Come lie there with your thorn:
For I'll be dead at the vesper-bell
    And buried the morrow morn.'

'There's blood on your lily breast, lady,
    Like roses when they blow,
And there's blood upon your little hand
    That should be white as snow:
I will stay amid my fellows
    Where the lilies grow.'

'But it's oh my own own little babe
    That I had you here to kiss,
And to comfort me in the strange next world
    Though I slighted you so in this.'

'You shall kiss both cheek and chin, mother,
    And kiss me between the eyes,
Or ever the moon is on her way
    And the pleasant stars arise:
You shall kiss and kiss your fill, mother,
    In the nest of Paradise.'

FROM THE ANTIQUE

It's a weary life, it is, she said:—
    Doubly blank in a woman's lot:
I wish and I wish I were a man:
    Or, better than any being, were not:

Were nothing at all in all the world,
    Not a body and not a soul:

Not so much as a grain of dust
    Or drop of water from pole to pole.

Still the world would wag on the same,
    Still the seasons go and come:
Blossom and bloom as in days of old,
    Cherries ripen and wild bees hum.

None would miss me in all the world,
    How much less would care or weep:
I should be nothing, while all the rest
    Would wake and weary and fall asleep.

LISTENING

She listened like a cushat dove
    That listens to its mate alone:
She listened like a cushat dove
    That loves but only one.

Not fair as men would reckon fair,
Nor noble as they count the line:
Only as graceful as a bough,
    And tendrils of the vine:
Only as noble as sweet Eve
    Your ancestress and mine.

And downcast were her dovelike eyes
And downcast was her tender cheek;
Her pulses fluttered like a dove
    To hear him speak.

ECHO

Come to me in the silence of the night;
   Come in the speaking silence of a dream;
Come with soft rounded cheeks and eyes as bright
   As sunlight on a stream;
     Come back in tears,
O memory, hope, love of finished years.

O dream how sweet, too sweet, too bitter sweet,
   Whose wakening should have been in Paradise,
Where souls brimfull of love abide and meet;
   Where thirsting longing eyes
     Watch the slow door
That opening, letting in, lets out no more.

Yet come to me in dreams, that I may live
   My very life again though cold in death:
Come back to me in dreams, that I may give
   Pulse for pulse, breath for breath:
     Speak low, lean low,
As long ago, my love, how long ago.

THE FIRST SPRING DAY

I wonder if the sap is stirring yet,
If wintry birds are dreaming of a mate,
If frozen snowdrops feel as yet the sun
And crocus fires are kindling one by one:
   Sing, robin, sing;
I still am sore in doubt concerning Spring.

I wonder if the Springtide of this year
Will bring another Spring both lost and dear;
If heart and spirit will find out their Spring,
Or if the world alone will bud and sing:
     Sing, hope, to me;
Sweet notes, my hope, soft notes for memory.

The sap will surely quicken soon or late,
The tardiest bird will twitter to a mate;
So Spring must dawn again with warmth and bloom,
Or in this world or in the world to come:
     Sing, voice of Spring,
Till I too blossom and rejoice and sing.

MY DREAM

Hear now a curious dream I dreamed last night,
Each word whereof is weighed and sifted truth.

I stood beside Euphrates while it swelled
Like overflowing Jordan in its youth.
It waxed and coloured sensibly to sight;
Till out of myriad pregnant waves there welled
Young crocodiles, a gaunt blunt-featured crew,
Fresh-hatched perhaps and daubed with birthday dew.
The rest if I should tell, I fear my friend,
My closest friend, would deem the facts untrue;
And therefore it were wisely left untold;
Yet if you will, why, hear it to the end.

Each crocodile was girt with massive gold
And polished stones that with their wearers grew:
But one there was who waxed beyond the rest,

Wore kinglier girdle and a kingly crown,
Whilst crowns and orbs and sceptres starred his breast.
All gleamed compact and green with scale on scale,
But special burnishment adorned his mail
And special terror weighed upon his frown;
His punier brethren quaked before his tail,
Broad as a rafter, potent as a flail.
So he grew lord and master of his kin:
But who shall tell the tale of all their woes?
An execrable appetite arose,
He battened on them, crunched, and sucked them in.
He knew no law, he feared no binding law,
But ground them with inexorable jaw.
The luscious fat distilled upon his chin,
Exuded from his nostrils and his eyes,
While still like hungry death he fed his maw;
Till, every minor crocodile being dead
And buried too, himself gorged to the full,
He slept with breath oppressed and unstrung claw.

Oh marvel passing strange which next I saw!
In sleep he dwindled to the common size,
And all the empire faded from his coat.
Then from far off a wingèd vessel came,
Swift as a swallow, subtle as a flame:
I know not what it bore of freight or host,
But white it was as an avenging ghost.
It levelled strong Euphrates in its course;
Supreme yet weightless as an idle mote
It seemed to tame the waters without force
Till not a murmur swelled or billow beat.
Lo, as the purple shadow swept the sands,
The prudent crocodile rose on his feet,
And shed appropriate tears and wrung his hands.

What can it mean? you ask. I answer not
For meaning, but myself must echo, What?
And tell it as I saw it on the spot.

THE LAST LOOK

Her face was like an opening rose,
　　So bright to look upon:
But now it is like fallen snows,
　　As cold, as dead, as wan.

Heaven lit with stars is more like her
　　Than is the empty crust:
Deaf, dumb, and blind, it cannot stir,
　　But crumbles back to dust.

No flower be taken from her bed
　　For me, no lock be shorn:
I give her up, the early dead,
　　The dead, the newly born.

If I remember her, no need
　　Of formal tokens set;
Of hollow token-lies indeed
　　No need, if I forget.

MAY

I cannot tell you how it was;
But this I know: it came to pass—
Upon a bright and breezy day
When May was young, ah pleasant May!

As yet the poppies were not born
Between the blades of tender corn;
The last eggs had not hatched as yet,
Nor any bird forgone its mate.

I cannot tell you what it was;
But this I know: it did but pass.
It passed away with sunny May,
With all sweet things it passed away,
And left me old, and cold, and grey.

OLD AND NEW YEAR DITTIES

1

New Year met me somewhat sad:
   Old year leaves me tired,
Stripped of favourite things I had,
   Baulked of much desired:
Yet farther on my road to-day,
God willing, farther on my way.

New Year coming on apace,
   What have you to give me?
Bring you scathe or bring you grace,
Face me with an honest face:
   You shall not deceive me:
Be it good or ill, be it what you will,
It needs shall help me on my road,
My rugged way to heaven, please God.

2

Watch with me, men, women, and children dear,
You whom I love, for whom I hope and fear,

Watch with me this last vigil of the year.
Some hug their business, some their pleasure scheme;
Some seize the vacant hour to sleep or dream;
Heart locked in heart some kneel and watch apart.

Watch with me, blessed spirits, who delight
All through the holy night to walk in white,
Or take your ease after the long-drawn fight.
I know not if they watch with me: I know
They count this eve of resurrection slow,
And cry 'How long?' with urgent utterance strong.

Watch with me, Jesus, in my loneliness:
Though others say me nay, yet say Thou yes;
Though others pass me by, stop Thou to bless.
Yea, Thou dost stop with me this vigil night;
To-night of pain, to-morrow of delight:
I, Love, am Thine; Thou, Lord my God, art mine.

3

Passing away, saith the World, passing away:
Chances, beauty, and youth, sapped day by day:
Thy life never continueth in one stay.
Is the eye waxen dim, is the dark hair changing to grey
That hath won neither laurel nor bay?
I shall clothe myself in Spring and bud in May:
Thou, root-stricken, shalt not rebuild thy decay
On my bosom for aye.
Then I answered: Yea.

Passing away, saith my Soul, passing away:
With its burden of fear and hope, of labour and play,
Hearken what the past doth witness and say:
Rust in thy gold, a moth is in thine array,

A canker is in thy bud, thy leaf must decay.
At midnight, at cockcrow, at morning, one certain day
Lo the Bridegroom shall come and shall not delay;
Watch thou and pray.
Then I answered: Yea.

Passing away, saith my God, passing away:
Winter passeth after the long delay:
New grapes on the vine, new figs on the tender spray,
Turtle calleth turtle in Heaven's May.
Though I tarry, wait for Me, trust Me, watch and pray:
Arise, come away, night is past and lo it is day,
My love, My sister, My spouse, thou shalt hear Me say.
Then I answered: Yea.

SHUT OUT

The door was shut. I looked between
   Its iron bars; and saw it lie,
   My garden, mine, beneath the sky,
Pied with all flowers bedewed and green.

From bough to bough the song-birds crossed,
   From flower to flower the moths and bees:
   With all its nests and stately trees
It had been mine, and it was lost.

A shadowless spirit kept the gate,
   Blank and unchanging like the grave.
   I, peering through, said; 'Let me have
Some buds to cheer my outcast state.'

He answered not. 'Or give me, then,
   But one small twig from shrub or tree;

And bid my home remember me
Until I come to it again.'

The spirit was silent; but he took
   Mortar and stone to build a wall;
   He left no loophole great or small
Through which my straining eyes might look.

So now I sit here quite alone,
   Blinded with tears; nor grieve for that,
   For nought is left worth looking at
Since my delightful land is gone.

A violet bed is budding near,
   Wherein a lark has made her nest;
   And good they are, but not the best;
And dear they are, but not so dear.

A CHILLY NIGHT

I rose at the dead of night,
   And went to the lattice alone
To look for my Mother's ghost
   Where the ghostly moonlight shone.

My friends had failed one by one,
   Middle-aged, young, and old,
Till the ghosts were warmer to me
   Than my friends that had grown cold.

I looked and I saw the ghosts
   Dotting plain and mound:
They stood in the blank moonlight,

59

But no shadow lay on the ground:
They spoke without a voice
   And they leaped without a sound.

I called: 'O my Mother dear,'—
   I sobbed: 'O my Mother kind,
Make a lonely bed for me
   And shelter it from the wind.

'Tell the others not to come
   To see me night or day:
But I need not tell my friends
   To be sure to keep away.'

My Mother raised her eyes,
   They were blank and could not see:
Yet they held me with their stare
   While they seemed to look at me.

She opened her mouth and spoke;
   I could not hear a word,
While my flesh crept on my bones
   And every hair was stirred.

She knew that I could not hear
   The message that she told
Whether I had long to wait
   Or soon should sleep in the mould:
I saw her toss her shadowless hair
   And wring her hands in the cold.

I strained to catch her words,
   And she strained to make me hear;
But never a sound of words
   Fell on my straining ear.

From midnight to the cockcrow
   I kept my watch in pain
While the subtle ghosts grew subtler
   In the sad night on the wane.

From midnight to the cockcrow
   I watched till all were gone,
Some to sleep in the shifting sea
   And some under turf and stone:
Living had failed and dead had failed,
   And I was indeed alone.

IN THE LANE

When my love came home to me,
   Pleasant summer bringing,
Every tree was out in leaf,
   Every bird was singing.

There I met her in the lane
   By those waters gleamy,
Met her toward the fall of day,
   Warm and dear and dreamy.
Did I loiter in the lane?
   None was there to see me.

Only roses in the hedge,
   Lilies on the river,
Saw our greeting fast and fond,
   Counted gift and giver,
Saw me take her to my home,
   Take her home for ever.

A BED OF FORGET-ME-NOTS

Is Love so prone to change and rot
We are fain to rear Forget-me-not
By measure in a garden-plot?—

I love its growth at large and free
By untrod path and unlopped tree,
Or nodding by the unpruned hedge,
Or on the water's dangerous edge
Where flags and meadowsweet blow rank
With rushes on the quaking bank.

Love is not taught in learning's school,
Love is not parcelled out by rule:
Hath curb or call an answer got?—
So free must be Forget-me-not.
Give me the flame no dampness dulls,
The passion of the instinctive pulse,
Love steadfast as a fixèd star,
Tender as doves with nestlings are,
More large than time, more strong than death:
    This all creation travails of—
She groans not for a passing breath—
    This is Forget-me-not and Love.

LOVE FROM THE NORTH

I had a love in soft south land,
    Beloved through April far in May;
He waited on my lightest breath,
    And never dared to say me nay.

He saddened if my cheer was sad,
    But gay he grew if I was gay;
We never differed on a hair,
    My yes his yes, my nay his nay.

The wedding hour was come, the aisles
    Were flushed with sun and flowers that day;
I pacing balanced in my thoughts:
    'It's quite too late to think of nay.'—

My bridegroom answered in his turn,
    Myself had almost answered 'yea':
When through the flashing nave I heard
    A struggle and resounding 'nay'.

Bridemaids and bridegroom shrank in fear,
    But I stood high who stood at bay:
'And if I answer yea, fair Sir,
    What man art thou to bar with nay?'

He was a strong man from the north,
    Light-locked, with eyes of dangerous grey:
'Put yea by for another time
    In which I will not say thee nay.'

He took me in his strong white arms,
    He bore me on his horse away
O'er crag, morass, and hairbreadth pass,
    But never asked me yea or nay.

He made me fast with book and bell,
    With links of love he makes me stay;
Till now I've neither heart nor power
    Nor will nor wish to say him nay.

A BETTER RESURRECTION

I have no wit, no words, no tears;
  My heart within me like a stone
Is numbed too much for hopes or fears.
  Look right, look left, I dwell alone;
I lift mine eyes, but dimmed with grief
  No everlasting hills I see;
My life is in the falling leaf:
    O Jesus, quicken me.

My life is like a faded leaf,
  My harvest dwindled to a husk:
Truly my life is void and brief
  And tedious in the barren dusk;
My life is like a frozen thing,
  No bud nor greenness can I see;
Yet rise it shall—the sap of Spring:
    O Jesus, rise in me.

My life is like a broken bowl,
  A broken bowl that cannot hold
One drop of water for my soul
  Or cordial in the searching cold:
Cast in the fire the perished thing;
  Melt and remould it, till it be
A royal cup for Him, my King:
    O Jesus, drink of me.

THE HEART KNOWETH ITS OWN BITTERNESS

When all the over-work of life
  Is finished once, and fast asleep

We swerve no more beneath the knife
    But taste that silence cool and deep;
Forgetful of the highways rough,
    Forgetful of the thorny scourge,
    Forgetful of the tossing surge,
Then shall we find it is enough?

How can we say 'enough' on earth—
    'Enough' with such a craving heart?
I have not found it since my birth,
    But still have bartered part for part.
I have not held and hugged the whole,
    But paid the old to gain the new:
    Much have I paid, yet much is due,
Till I am beggared sense and soul.

I used to labour, used to strive
    For pleasure with a restless will:
Now if I save my soul alive
    All else what matters, good or ill?
I used to dream alone, to plan
    Unspoken hopes and days to come:—
    Of all my past this is the sum—
I will not lean on child of man.

To give, to give, not to receive!
    I long to pour myself, my soul,
Not to keep back or count or leave,
    But king with king to give the whole.
I long for one to stir my deep—
    I have had enough of help and gift—
    I long for one to search and sift
Myself, to take myself and keep.

You scratch my surface with your pin,
　　You stroke me smooth with hushing breath:—
Nay pierce, nay probe, nay dig within,
　　Probe my quick core and sound my depth.
You call me with a puny call,
　　You talk, you smile, you nothing do:
　　How should I spend my heart on you,
My heart that so outweighs you all?

Your vessels are by much too strait:
　　Were I to pour, you could not hold.—
Bear with me: I must bear to wait,
　　A fountain sealed through heat and cold.
Bear with me days or months or years:
　　Deep must call deep until the end
　　When friend shall no more envy friend
Nor vex his friend at unawares.

Not in this world of hope deferred,
　　This world of perishable stuff:—
Eye hath not seen nor ear hath heard
　　Nor heart conceived that full 'enough':
Here moans the separating sea,
　　Here harvests fail, here breaks the heart:
　　There God shall join and no man part,
I full of Christ and Christ of me.

FATA MORGANA

A blue-eyed phantom far before
　　Is laughing, leaping toward the sun:
Like lead I chase it evermore,
　　I pant and run.

It breaks the sunlight bound on bound:
    Goes singing as it leaps along
To sheep-bells with a dreamy sound
    A dreamy song.

I laugh, it is so brisk and gay;
    It is so far before, I weep:
I hope I shall lie down some day,
    Lie down and sleep.

ONE DAY

I will tell you when they met:
In the limpid days of Spring;
Elder boughs were budding yet,
Oaken boughs looked wintry still,
But primrose and veined violet
In the mossful turf were set,
While meeting birds made haste to sing
And build with right good will.

I will tell you when they parted;
When plenteous Autumn sheaves were brown
Then they parted heavy-hearted;
The full rejoicing sun looked down
As grand as in the days before;
Only they had lost a crown;
Only to them those days of yore
Could come back nevermore.

When shall they meet? I cannot tell,
Indeed, when they shall meet again,
Except some day in Paradise:

For this they wait, one waits in pain.
Beyond the sea of death Love lies
For ever, yesterday, to-day;
Angels shall ask them, 'Is it well?'
And they shall answer 'Yea'.

INTROSPECTIVE

I wish it were over the terrible pain,
Pang after pang again and again:
First the shattering ruining blow,
Then the probing steady and slow.

Did I wince? I did not faint:
My soul broke but was not bent:
Up I stand like a blasted tree
By the shore of the shivering sea.

On my boughs neither leaf nor fruit,
No sap in my uttermost root,
Brooding in an anguish dumb
On the short past and the long to-come.

Dumb I was when the ruin fell,
Dumb I remain and will never tell;
O my soul, I talk with thee,
But not another the sight must see.

I did not start when the torture stung,
I did not faint when the torture wrung:
Let it come tenfold if come it must,
But I will not groan when I bite the dust.

IN THE ROUND TOWER AT JHANSI
8 June 1857

A hundred, a thousand to one; even so;
    Not a hope in the world remained:
The swarming howling wretches below
    Gained and gained and gained.

Skene looked at his pale young wife.
    'Is the time come?'—'The time is come.'
Young, strong, and so full of life,
    The agony struck them dumb.

Close his arm about her now,
    Close her cheek to his,
Close the pistol to her brow—
    God forgive them this!

'Will it hurt much?'—'No, mine own:
    I wish I could bear the pang for both.'—
'I wish I could bear the pang alone:
    Courage, dear, I am not loth.'

Kiss and kiss: 'It is not pain
    Thus to kiss and die.
One kiss more.'—'And yet one again.'—
    'Good-bye.'—'Good-bye.'

MEMORY

1

I nursed it in my bosom while it lived,
    I hid it in my heart when it was dead.

69

In joy I sat alone; even so I grieved
    Alone, and nothing said.

I shut the door to face the naked truth,
    I stood alone—I faced the truth alone,
Stripped bare of self-regard or forms or ruth
    Till first and last were shown.

I took the perfect balances and weighed;
    No shaking of my hand disturbed the poise;
Weighed, found it wanting: not a word I said,
    But silent made my choice.

None know the choice I made; I make it still.
    None know the choice I made and broke my heart,
Breaking mine idol: I have braced my will
    Once, chosen for once my part.

I broke it at a blow, I laid it cold,
    Crushed in my deep heart where it used to live.
My heart dies inch by inch; the time grows old,
    Grows old in which I grieve.

2

I have a room whereinto no one enters
    Save I myself alone:
    There sits a blessed memory on a throne,
There my life centres;

While winter comes and goes—oh tedious comer!—
    And while its nip-wind blows;
    While bloom the bloodless lily and warm rose
Of lavish summer.

If any should force entrance he might see there
    One buried yet not dead,
    Before whose face I no more bow my head
Or bend my knee there;

But often in my worn life's autumn weather
    I watch there with clear eyes,
    And think how it will be in Paradise
When we're together.

A BIRTHDAY

My heart is like a singing bird
    Whose nest is in a watered shoot:
My heart is like an apple-tree
    Whose boughs are bent with thickset fruit;
My heart is like a rainbow shell
    That paddles in a halcyon sea;
My heart is gladder than all these
    Because my love is come to me.

Raise me a dais of silk and down;
    Hang it with vair and purple dyes;
Carve it in doves and pomegranates,
    And peacocks with a hundred eyes;
Work it in gold and silver grapes,
    In leaves and silver fleurs-de-lys;
Because the birthday of my life
    Is come, my love is come to me.

AN APPLE GATHERING

I plucked pink blossoms from mine apple-tree
    And wore them all that evening in my hair:
Then in due season when I went to see
    I found no apples there.

With dangling basket all along the grass
    As I had come I went the self-same track:
My neighbours mocked me while they saw me pass
    So empty-handed back.

Lilian and Lilias smiled in trudging by,
    Their heaped-up basket teazed me like a jeer;
Sweet-voiced they sang beneath the sunset sky,
    Their mother's home was near.

Plump Gertrude passed me with her basket full,
    A stronger hand than hers helped it along
A voice talked with her through the shadows cool
    More sweet to me than song.

Ah Willie, Willie, was my love less worth
    Than apples with their green leaves piled above?
I counted rosiest apples on the earth
    Of far less than love.

So once it was with me you stooped to talk
    Laughing and listening in this very lane;
To think that by this way we used to walk
    We shall not walk again!

I let my neighbours pass me, ones and twos
    And groups; the latest said the night grew chill,

And hastened: but I loitered; while the dews
    Fell fast I loitered still.

WINTER: MY SECRET

I tell my secret? No indeed, not I:
Perhaps some day, who knows?
But not to-day; it froze, and blows, and snows
And you're too curious: fie!
You want to hear it? well:
Only, my secret's mine, and I won't tell.

Or, after all, perhaps there's none:
Suppose there is no secret after all,
But only just my fun.
To-day's a nipping day, a biting day;
In which one wants a shawl,
A veil, a cloak, and other wraps:
I cannot ope to every one who taps,
And let the draughts come whistling through my hall;
Come bounding and surrounding me,
Come buffeting, astounding me,
Nipping and clipping through my wraps and all.
I wear my mask for warmth: who ever shows
His nose to Russian snows
To be pecked at by every wind that blows?
You would not peck? I thank you for good will,
Believe, but leave that truth untested still.

Spring's an expansive time: yet I don't trust
March with its peck of dust,
Nor April with its rainbow-crowned brief showers,
Nor even May, whose flowers
One frost may wither through the sunless hours.

Perhaps some languid summer day,
When drowsy birds sing less and less,
And golden fruit is ripening to excess,
If there's not much sun nor too much cloud,
And the warm wind is neither still nor loud,
Perhaps my secret I may say,
Or you may guess.

MY FRIEND

Two days ago with dancing glancing hair,
  With living lips and eyes;
  Now pale, dumb, blind, she lies;
So pale, yet still so fair.

We have not left her yet, not yet alone;
  But soon must leave her where
  She will not miss our care,
Bone of our bone.

Weep not, O friends, we should not weep:
  Our friend of friends lies full of rest;
  No sorrow rankles in her breast,
Fallen fast asleep.

She sleeps below,
  She wakes and laughs above.
  To-day, as she walked, let us walk in love:
To-morrow follow so.

ANOTHER SPRING

If I might see another Spring,
   I'd not plant summer flowers and wait:
I'd have my crocuses at once,
My leafless pink mezereons,
   My chill-veined snowdrops, choicer yet
   My white or azure violet,
Leaf-nested primrose; anything
   To blow at once, not late.

If I might see another Spring,
   I'd listen to the daylight birds
That build their nests and pair and sing,
Nor wait for mateless nightingale;
   I'd listen to the lusty herds,
   The ewes with lambs as white as snow,
I'd find out music in the hail
   And all the winds that blow.

If I might see another Spring—
   Oh stinging comment on my past
That all my past results in 'if'—
   If I might see another Spring
I'd laugh to-day, to-day is brief;
I would not wait for anything:
   I'd use to-day that cannot last,
   Be glad to-day and sing.

UP-HILL

Does the road wind up-hill all the way?
   Yes, to the very end.

Will the day's journey take the whole long day?
    From morn to night, my friend.

But is there for the night a resting-place?
    A roof for when the slow dark hours begin.
May not the darkness hide it from my face?
    You cannot miss that inn.

Shall I meet other wayfarers at night?
    Those who have gone before.
Then must I knock, or call when just in sight?
    They will not keep you standing at that door.

Shall I find comfort, travel-sore and weak?
    Of labour you shall find the sum.
Will there be beds for me and all who seek?
    Yea, beds for all who come.

AT HOME

When I was dead, my spirit turned
    To seek the much-frequented house.
I passed the door, and saw my friends
    Feasting beneath green orange-boughs;
From hand to hand they pushed the wine,
    They sucked the pulp of plum and peach;
They sang, they jested, and they laughed,
    For each was loved of each.

I listened to their honest chat.
    Said one: 'To-morrow we shall be
Plod plod along the featureless sands,
    And coasting miles and miles of sea.'

Said one: 'Before the turn of tide
  We will achieve the eyrie-seat.'
Said one: 'To-morrow shall be like
  To-day, but much more sweet.'

'To-morrow,' said they, strong with hope,
  And dwelt upon the pleasant way:
'To-morrow,' cried they one and all,
  While no one spoke of yesterday.
Their life stood full at blessed noon;
  I, only I, had passed away:
  'To-morrow and to-day,' they cried;
  I was of yesterday.

I shivered comfortless, but cast
  No chill across the tablecloth;
I all-forgotten shivered, sad
  To stay and yet to part how loth:
I passed from the familiar room,
  I who from love had passed away,
Like the remembrance of a guest
  That tarrieth but a day.

TO-DAY AND TO-MORROW

1

All the world is out in leaf,
  Half the world in flower,
Earth has waited weeks and weeks
  For this special hour:
Faint the rainbow comes and goes
  On a sunny shower.

77

All the world is making love:
　　Bird to bird in bushes,
Beast to beast in glades, and frog
　　To frog among the rushes:
Wake, O south wind sweet with spice,
　　Wake the rose to blushes.

Life breaks forth to right and left—
　　Pipe wild-wood notes cheery.
Nevertheless there are the dead
　　Fast asleep and weary—
To-day we live, to-day we love,
　　Wake and listen, deary.

2

　　I wish I were dead, my foe,
　　My friend, I wish I were dead,
　　With a stone at my tired feet
　　And a stone at my tired head.

In the pleasant April days
Half the world will stir and sing,
But half the world will slug and rot
　　For all the sap of Spring.

YET A LITTLE WHILE

These days are long before I die:
　　To sit alone upon a thorn
　　Is what the nightingale forlorn
Does night by night continually:
She swells her heart to ecstasy
Until it bursts and she can die.

78

These days are long that wane and wax:
    Waxeth and wanes the ghostly moon,
    Achill and pale in cordial June:
What is it that she wandering lacks?
She seems as one that aches and aches,
Most sick to wane, most sick to wax.

Of all the sad sights in the world
    The downfall of an Autumn leaf
    Is grievous and suggesteth grief:
Who thought when Spring was fresh unfurled
Of this? when Spring-twigs gleamed impearled
Who thought of frost that nips the world?

There are a hundred subtle stings
    To prick us in our daily walk:
    A young fruit cankered on its stalk,
A strong bird snared for all his wings,
A nest that sang but never sings:
Yea sight and sound and silence stings.

There is a lack in solitude,
    There is a load in throng of life:
    One with another genders strife,
To be alone yet is not good:
I know but of one neighbourhood
At peace and full—death's solitude.

Sleep soundly, dears, who lulled at last
    Forget the bird and all her pains,
    Forget the moon that waxes, wanes,
The leaf, the sting, the frostful blast:
Forget the troublous years that, past
In strife or ache, did end at last.

We have clear call of daily bells,
   A dimness where the anthems are,
   A chancel vault of sky and star,
A thunder if the organ swells:
Alas our daily life—what else?—
Is not in tune with daily bells.

You have deep pause betwixt the chimes
   Of earth and heaven, a patient pause
   Yet glad with rest by certain laws:
You look and long: while oftentimes
Precursive flush of morning climbs,
And air vibrates with coming chimes.

GOBLIN MARKET

Morning and evening
Maids heard the goblins cry
'Come buy our orchard fruits,
Come buy, come buy:
Apples and quinces,
Lemons and oranges,
Plump unpecked cherries,
Melons and raspberries,
Bloom-down-cheeked peaches,
Swart-headed mulberries,
Wild free-born cranberries,
Crab-apples, dewberries,
Pine-apples, blackberries,
Apricots, strawberries;—
All ripe together
In summer weather,—
Morns that pass by,

Fair eves that fly;
Come buy, come buy:
Our grapes fresh from the vine,
Pomegranates full and fine,
Dates and sharp bullaces,
Rare pears and greengages,
Damsons and bilberries,
Taste them and try:
Currants and gooseberries,
Bright-fire-like barberries,
Figs to fill your mouth,
Citrons from the South,
Sweet to tongue and sound to eye;
Come buy, come buy.'

Evening by evening
Among the brookside rushes,
Laura bowed her head ro hear,
Lizzie veiled her blushes:
Crouching close together
In the cooling weather,
With clasping arms and cautioning lips,
With tingling cheeks and finger tips.
'Lie close,' Laura said,
Pricking up her golden head:
'We must not look at goblin men,
We must not buy their fruits:
Who knows upon what soil they fed
Their hungry thirsty roots?'
'Come buy,' call the goblins
Hobbling down the glen.
'Oh,' cried Lizzie, 'Laura, Laura,
You should not peep at goblin men.'
Lizzie covered up her eyes,

Covered close lest they should look;
Laura reared her glossy head,
And whispered like the restless brook:
'Look, Lizzie, look, Lizzie,
Down the glen tramp little men.
One hauls a basket,
One bears a plate,
One lugs a golden dish
Of many pounds' weight.
How fair the vine must grow
Whose grapes are so luscious;
How warm the wind must blow
Through those fruit bushes.'

'No,' said Lizzie, 'No, no, no;
Their offers should not charm us,
Their evil gifts would harm us.'
She thrust a dimpled finger
In each ear, shut eyes and ran:
Curious Laura chose to linger
Wondering at each merchant man.
One had a cat's face,
One whisked a tail,
One tramped at a rat's pace,
One crawled like a snail,
One like a wombat prowled obtuse and furry,
One like a ratel tumbled hurry skurry.
She heard a voice like voice of doves
Cooing all together:
They sounded kind and full of loves
In the pleasant weather.

Laura stretched her gleaming neck
Like a rush-imbedded swan,

Like a lily from the beck,
Like a moonlit poplar branch,
Like a vessel at the launch
When its last restraint is gone.

Backwards up the mossy glen
Turned and trooped the goblin men,
With their shrill repeated cry,
'Come buy, come buy.'
When they reached where Laura was
They stood stock still upon the moss,
Leering at each other,
Brother with queer brother;
Signalling each other,
Brother with sly brother.
One set his basket down,
One reared his plate;
One began to weave a crown
Of tendrils, leaves, and rough nuts brown
(Men sell not such in any town);
One heaved the golden weight
Of dish and fruit to offer her:
'Come buy, come buy,' was still their cry.
Laura stared but did not stir,
Longed but had no money.
The whisk-tailed merchant bade her taste
In tones as smooth as honey,
The cat-faced purr'd,
The rat-paced spoke a word
Of welcome, and the snail-paced even was heard;
One parrot-voiced and jolly
Cried 'Pretty Goblin' still for 'Pretty Polly';
One whistled like a bird.

But sweet-tooth Laura spoke in haste:
'Good Folk, I have no coin;
To take were to purloin:
I have no copper in my purse,
I have no silver either,
And all my gold is on the furze
That shakes in windy weather
Above the rusty heather.'
'You have much gold upon your head,'
They answered all together:
'Buy from us with a golden curl.'
She clipped a precious golden lock,
She dropped a tear more rare than pearl,
Then sucked their fruit-globes fair or red.
Sweeter than honey from the rock,
Stronger than man-rejoicing wine,
Clearer than water flowed that juice;
She never tasted such before,
How should it cloy with length of use?
She sucked and sucked and sucked the more
Fruits which that unknown orchard bore;
She sucked until her lips were sore;
Then flung the emptied rinds away
But gathered up one kernel stone,
And knew not was it night or day
As she turned home alone.

Lizzie met her at the gate
Full of wise upbraidings:
'Dear, you should not stay so late,
Twilight is not good for maidens;
Should not loiter in the glen
In the haunts of goblin men.
Do you not remember Jeanie,

How she met them in the moonlight,
Took their gifts both choice and many,
Ate their fruits and wore their flowers
Plucked from bowers
Where summer ripens at all hours?
But ever in the noonlight
She pined and pined away;
Sought them by night and day,
Found them no more, but dwindled and grew grey;
Then fell with the first snow,
While to this day no grass will grow
Where she lies low:
I planted daisies there a year ago
That never blow.
You should not loiter so.'
'Nay, hush,' said Laura:
'Nay, hush, my sister:
I ate and ate my fill,
Yet my mouth waters still:
To-morrow night I will
Buy more;' and kissed her.
'Have done with sorrow;
I'll bring you plums to-morrow
Fresh on their mother twigs,
Cherries worth getting;
You cannot think what figs
My teeth have met in,
What melons icy-cold
Piled on a dish of gold
Too huge for me to hold,
What peaches with a velvet nap,
Pellucid grapes without one seed:
Odorous indeed must be the mead
Whereon they grow, and pure the wave they drink

With lilies at the brink,
And sugar-sweet their sap.'

Golden head by golden head,
Like two pigeons in one nest
Folded in each other's wings,
They lay down in their curtained bed:
Like two blossoms on one stem,
Like two flakes of new-fall'n snow,
Like two wands of ivory
Tipped with gold for awful kings.
Moon and stars gazed in at them,
Wind sang to them a lullaby,
Lumbering owls forebore to fly,
Not a bat flapped to and fro
Round their nest:
Cheek to cheek and breast to breast
Locked together in one nest.

Early in the morning
When the first cock crowed his warning,
Neat like bees, as sweet and busy,
Laura rose with Lizzie:
Fetched in honey, milked the cows,
Aired and set to rights the house,
Kneaded cakes of whitest wheat,
Cakes for dainty mouths to eat,
Next churned butter, whipped up cream,
Fed their poultry, sat and sewed;
Talked as modest maidens should:
Lizzie with an open heart,
Laura in an absent dream,
One content, one sick in part;
One warbling for the mere bright day's delight,
One longing for the night.

At length slow evening came:
They went with pitchers to the reedy brook;
Lizzie most placid in her look,
Laura most like a leaping flame.
They drew the gurgling water from its deep.
Lizzie plucked purple and rich golden flags,
Then turning homeward said: 'The sunset flushes
Those furthest loftiest crags;
Come, Laura, not another maiden lags.
No wilful squirrel wags,
The beasts and birds are fast asleep.'
But Laura loitered still among the rushes,
And said the bank was steep.

And said the hour was early still,
The dew not fall'n, the wind not chill;
Listening ever, but not catching
The customary cry,
'Come buy, come buy,'
With its iterated jingle
Of sugar-baited words:
Not for all her watching
Once discerning even one goblin.
Racing, whisking, tumbling, hobbling—
Let alone the herds
That used to tramp along the glen,
In groups or single,
Of brisk fruit-merchant men.

Till Lizzie urged, 'O Laura, come;
I hear the fruit-call, but I dare not look:
You should not loiter longer at this brook:
Come with me home.
The stars rise, the moon bends her arc,

Each glow-worm winks her spark,
Let us get home before the night grows dark:
For clouds may gather
Though this is summer weather,
Put out the lights and drench us through;
Then if we lost our way what should we do?

Laura turned cold as stone
To find her sister heard that cry alone,
That goblin cry,
'Come buy our fruits, come buy.'
Must she then buy no more such dainty fruit?
Must she no more such succous pasture find,
Gone deaf and blind?
Her tree of life drooped from the root:
She said not one word in her heart's sore ache:
But peering thro' the dimness, nought discerning,
Trudged home, her pitcher dripping all the way;
So crept to bed, and lay
Silent till Lizzie slept;
Then sat up in a passionate yearning,
And gnashed her teeth for baulked desire, and wept
As if her heart would break.

Day after day, night after night,
Laura kept watch in vain
In sullen silence of exceeding pain.
She never caught again the goblin cry,
 Come buy, come buy;'—
She never spied the goblin men
Hawking their fruits along the glen:
But when the noon waxed bright
Her hair grew thin and grey;
She dwindled, as the fair full moon doth turn

To swift decay and burn
Her fire away.

One day remembering her kernel-stone
She set it by a wall that faced the south;
Dewed it with tears, hoped for a root,
Watched for a waxing shoot,
But there came none.
It never saw the sun,
It never felt the trickling moisture run:
While with sunk eyes and faded mouth
She dreamed of melons, as a traveller sees
False waves in desert drouth
With shade of leaf-crowned trees,
And burns the thirstier in the sandful breeze.

She no more swept the house,
Tended the fowls or cows,
Fetched honey, kneaded cakes of wheat,
Brought water from the brook:
But sat down listless in the chimney-nook
And would not eat.

Tender Lizzie could not bear
To watch her sister's cankerous care,
Yet not to share.
She night and morning
Caught the goblins' cry:
'Come buy our orchard fruits,
Come buy, come buy:'—
Beside the brook, along the glen,
She heard the tramp of goblin men,
The voice and stir
Poor Laura could not hear;

Longed to buy fruit to comfort her,
But feared to pay too dear.
She thought of Jeanie in her grave,
Who should have been a bride;
But who for joys brides hope to have
Fell sick and died
In her gay prime,
In earliest winter time,
With the first glazing rime,
With the first snow-fall of crisp winter time.

Till Laura dwindling
Seemed knocking at Death's door.
Then Lizzie weighed no more
Better and worse;
But put a silver penny in her purse,
Kissed Laura, crossed the heath with clumps of furze
At twilight, halted by the brook:
And for the first time in her life
Began to listen and look.

Laughed every goblin
When they spied her peeping:
Came towards her hobbling,
Flying, running, leaping,
Puffing and blowing,
Chuckling, clapping, crowing,
Clucking and gobbling,
Mopping and mowing,
Full of airs and graces,
Pulling wry faces,
Demure grimaces,
Cat-like and rat-like,
Ratel- and wombat-like,

Snail-paced in a hurry,
Parrot-voiced and whistler,
Helter skelter, hurry skurry,
Chattering like magpies,
Fluttering like pigeons,
Gliding like fishes,—
Hugged her and kissed her:
Squeezed and caressed her:
Stretched up their dishes,
Panniers and plates:
'Look at our apples
Russet and dun,
Bob at our cherries,
Bite at our peaches,
Citrons and dates,
Grapes for the asking,
Pears red with basking
Out in the sun,
Plums on their twigs;
Pluck them and suck them,—
Pomegranates, figs.'

'Good folk,' said Lizzie,
Mindful of Jeanie:
'Give me much and many:'
Held out her apron,
Tossed them her penny.
'Nay, take a seat with us,
Honour and eat with us,'
They answered grinning:
'Our feast is but beginning.
Night yet is early,
Warm and dew-pearly,
Wakeful and starry:

91

Such fruits as these
No man can carry;
Half their bloom would fly,
Half their dew would dry,
Half their flavour would pass by.
Sit down and feast with us,
Be welcome guest with us,
Cheer you and rest with us.'—
'Thank you,' said Lizzie: 'But one waits
At home alone for me:
So without further parleying,
If you will not sell me any
Of your fruits though much and many,
Give me back my silver penny
I tossed you for a fee.'—
They began to scratch their pates,
No longer wagging, purring,
But visibly demurring,
Grunting and snarling.
One called her proud,
Cross-grained, uncivil;
Their tones waxed loud,
Their looks were evil.
Lashing their tails
They trod and hustled her,
Elbowed and jostled her,
Clawed with their nails,
Barking, mewing, hissing, mocking,
Tore her gown and soiled her stocking,
Twitched her hair out by the roots,
Stamped upon her tender feet,
Held her hands and squeezed their fruits
Against her mouth to make her eat.

White and golden Lizzie stood,
Like a lily in a flood,—
Like a rock of blue-veined stone
Lashed by tides obstreperously,—
Like a beacon left alone
In a hoary roaring sea,
Sending up a golden fire,—
Like a fruit-crowned orange-tree
White with blossoms honey-sweet
Sore beset by wasp and bee,—
Like a royal virgin town
Topped with gilded dome and spire
Close beleaguered by a fleet
Mad to tug her standard down.

One may lead a horse to water,
Twenty cannot make him drink.
Though the goblins cuffed and caught her,
Coaxed and fought her,
Bullied and besought her,
Scratched her, pinched her black as ink,
Kicked and knocked her,
Mauled and mocked her,
Lizzie uttered not a word;
Would not open lip from lip
Lest they should cram a mouthful in:
But laughed in heart to feel the drip
Of juice that syruped all her face,
And lodged in dimples of her chin,
And streaked her neck which quaked like curd.
At last the evil people,
Worn out by her resistance,
Flung back her penny, kicked their fruit
Along whichever road they took,

Not leaving root or stone or shoot;
Some writhed into the ground,
Some dived into the brook
With ring and ripple,
Some scudded on the gale without a sound,
Some vanished in the distance.

In a smart, ache, tingle,
Lizzie went her way;
Knew not was it night or day;
Sprang up the bank, tore thro' the furze,
Threaded copse and dingle,
And heard her penny jingle
Bouncing in her purse,—
Its bounce was music to her ear.
She ran and ran
As if she feared some goblin man
Dogged her with gibe or curse
Or something worse:
But not one goblin skurried after,
Nor was she pricked by fear;
The kind heart made her windy-paced
That urged her home quite out of breath with haste
And inward laughter.

She cried, 'Laura,' up the garden,
'Did you miss me?
Come and kiss me.
Never mind my bruises,
Hug me, kiss me, suck my juices
Squeezed from goblin fruits for you,
Goblin pulp and goblin dew.
Eat me, drink me, love me;
Laura, make much of me;

For your sake I have braved the glen
And had to do with goblin merchant men.'

Laura started from her chair,
Flung her arms up in the air,
Clutched her hair:
'Lizzie, Lizzie, have you tasted
For my sake the fruit forbidden?
Must your light like mine be hidden,
Your young life like mine be wasted,
Undone in my undoing,
And ruined in my ruin,
Thirsty, cankered, goblin-ridden?'—
She clung about her sister,
Kissed and kissed and kissed her:
Tears once again
Refreshed her shrunken eyes,
Dropping like rain
After long sultry drouth;
Shaking with aguish fear, and pain,
She kissed and kissed her with a hungry mouth.

Her lips began to scorch,
That juice was wormwood to her tongue,
She loathed the feast:
Writhing as one possessed she leaped and sung,
Rent all her robe, and wrung
Her hands in lamentable haste,
And beat her breast.
Her locks streamed like the torch
Borne by a racer at full speed,
Or like the mane of horses in their flight,
Or like an eagle when she stems the light
Straight toward the sun,

Or like a caged thing freed,
Or like a flying flag when armies run.

Swift fire spread through her veins, knocked at her heart,
Met the fire smouldering there
And overbore its lesser flame;
She gorged on bitterness without a name:
Ah fool, to choose such part
Of soul-consuming care!
Sense failed in the mortal strife:
Like the watch-tower of a town
Which an earthquake shatters down,
Like a lightning-stricken mast,
Like a wind-uprooted tree
Spun about,
Like a foam-topped waterspout
Cast down headlong in the sea,
She fell at last;
Pleasure past and anguish past,
Is it death or is it life?

Life out of death.
That night long Lizzie watched by her,
Counted her pulse's flagging stir,
Felt for her breath,
Held water to her lips, and cooled her face
With tears and fanning leaves.
But when the first birds chirped about their eaves,
And early reapers plodded to the place
Of golden sheaves,
And dew-wet grass
Bowed in the morning winds so brisk to pass,
And new buds with new day
Opened of cup-like lilies on the stream,

Laura awoke as from a dream,
Laughed in the innocent old way,
Hugged Lizzie but not twice or thrice;
Her gleaming locks showed not one thread of grey,
Her breath was sweet as May,
And light danced in her eyes.

Days, weeks, months, years
Afterwards, when both were wives
With children of their own;
Their mother-hearts beset with fears,
Their lives bound up in tender lives;
Laura would call the little ones
And tell them of her early prime,
Those pleasant days long gone
Of not-returning time:
Would talk about the haunted glen,
The wicked quaint fruit-merchant men,
Their fruits like honey to the throat
But poison in the blood
(Men sell not such in any town):
Would tell them how her sister stood
In deadly peril to do her good,
And win the fiery antidote:
Then joining hands to little hands
Would bid them cling together,—
'For there is no friend like a sister
In calm or stormy weather;
To cheer one on the tedious way,
To fetch one if one goes astray,
To lift one if one totters down,
To strengthen whilst one stands.'

L. E. L.
'Whose heart was breaking for a little love.'

Downstairs I laugh, I sport and jest with all;
    But in my solitary room above
I turn my face in silence to the wall;
    My heart is breaking for a little love.
        Though winter frosts are done,
        And birds pair every one,
And leaves peep out, for springtide is begun.

I feel no spring, while spring is well-nigh blown,
    I find no nest, while nests are in the grove:
Woe's me for mine own heart that dwells alone,
    My heart that breaketh for a little love.
        While golden in the sun
        Rivulets rise and run,
While lilies bud, for springtide is begun.

All love, are loved, save only I; their hearts
    Beat warm with love and joy, beat full thereof:
They cannot guess, who play the pleasant parts,
    My heart is breaking for a little love.
        While bee-hives wake and whirr,
        And rabbit thins his fur,
In living spring that sets the world astir.

I deck myself with silks and jewelry,
    I plume myself like any mated dove:
They praise my rustling show, and never see
    My heart is breaking for a little love.
        While sprouts green lavender
        With rosemary and myrrh,
For in quick spring the sap is all astir.

Perhaps some saints in glory guess the truth,
    Perhaps some angels read it as they move,
And cry one to another full of ruth,
    'Her heart is breaking for a little love.'
        Though other things have birth,
        And leap and sing for mirth,
When springtime wakes and clothes and feeds the earth.

Yet saith a saint, 'Take patience for thy scythe';
    Yet saith an angel: 'Wait, and thou shalt prove
True best is last, true life is born of death,
    O thou, heart-broken for a little love.
        Then love shall fill thy girth,
        And love make fat thy dearth,
When new spring builds new heaven and clean new earth.'

SPRING

Frost-locked all the winter,
Seeds, and roots, and stones of fruits,
What shall make their sap ascend
That they may put forth shoots?
Tips of tender green,
Leaf, or blade, or sheath;
Telling of the hidden life
That breaks forth underneath,
Life nursed in its grave by Death.

Blows the thaw-wind pleasantly,
Drips the soaking rain,
By fits looks down the waking sun:
Young grass springs on the plain;
Young leaves clothe early hedgerow trees;

99

Seeds, and roots, and stones of fruits,
Swoln with sap put forth their shoots;
Curled-headed ferns sprout in the lane;
Birds sing and pair again.

There is no time like Spring,
When life's alive in everything,
Before new nestlings sing,
Before cleft swallows speed their journey back
Along the trackless track—
God guides their wing,
He spreads their table that they nothing lack,—
Before the daisy grows a common flower,
Before the sun has power
To scorch the world up in his noontide hour.

There is no time like Spring,
Like Spring that passes by;
There is no life like Spring-life born to die,—
Piercing the sod,
Clothing the uncouth clod,
Hatched in the nest,
Fledged on the windy bough,
Strong on the wing:
There is no time like Spring that passes by,
Now newly born, and now
Hastening to die.

WHAT GOOD SHALL MY LIFE DO ME?

No hope in life: yet is there hope
In death, the threshold of man's scope.
Man yearneth (as the heliotrope

For ever seeks the sun) through light,
Through dark, for Love: all, read aright,
Is Love, for Love is infinite.

Shall not this infinite Love suffice
To feed thy dearth? Lift heart and eyes
Up to the hills, grow glad and wise.

The hills are glad because the sun
Kisses their round tops every one
Where silver fountains laugh and run:

Smooth pebbles shine beneath: beside,
The grass, mere green, grows myriad-eyed
With pomp of blossoms veined or pied.

So every nest is glad whereon
The sun in tender strength has shone:
So every fruit he glows upon:

So every valley depth, whose herds
At pasture praise him without words:
So the winged ecstasies of birds.

If there be any such thing, what
Is there by sunlight betters not?
Nothing except dead things that rot.

Thou then who art not dead, and fit,
Like blasted tree beside the pit,
But for the axe that levels it,

Living show life of Love, whereof
The force wields earth and heaven above:
Who knows not Love begetteth Love?

Love in the gracious rain distils:
Love moves the subtle fountain-rills
To fertilize uplifted hills,

And seedful valleys fertilize:
Love stills the hungry lion's cries,
And the young raven satisfies:

Love hangs this earth in space: Love rolls
Fair worlds rejoicing on their poles,
And girds them round with aureoles:

Love lights the sun: Love through the dark
Lights the moon's evanescent arc:
Same Love lights up the glow-worm's spark:

Love rears the great: Love tends the small:
Breaks off the yoke, breaks down the wall:
Accepteth all, fulfilleth all.

O ye who taste that Love is sweet,
Set waymarks for the doubtful feet
That stumble on in search of it.

Sing hymns of Love, that those who hear
Far off in pain may lend an ear,
Rise up and wonder and draw near.

Lead lives of Love, that others who
Behold your lives may kindle too
With Love and cast their lots with you.

COUSIN KATE

I was a cottage-maiden
 Hardened by sun and air,
Contented with my cottage-mates,
 Not mindful I was fair.
Why did a great lord find me out
 And praise my flaxen hair?
Why did a great lord find me out
 To fill my heart with care?

He lured me to his palace-home—
 Woe's me for joy thereof—
To lead a shameless shameful life,
 His plaything and his love.
He wore me like a golden knot,
 He changed me like a glove:
So now I moan an unclean thing
 Who might have been a dove.

O Lady Kate, my Cousin Kate,
 You grow more fair than I:
He saw you at your father's gate,
 Chose you and cast me by.
He watched your steps along the lane,
 Your sport among the rye:
He lifted you from mean estate
 To sit with him on high.

Because you were so good and pure
 He bound you with his ring:
The neighbours call you good and pure,
 Call me an outcast thing.
Even so I sit and howl in dust

You sit in gold and sing:
Now which of us has tenderer heart?
    You had the stronger wing.

O Cousin Kate, my love was true,
    Your love was writ in sand:
If he had fooled not me but you,
    If you stood where I stand,
He had not won me with his love
    Nor bought me with his land:
I would have spit into his face
    And not have taken his hand.

Yet I've a gift you have not got
    And seem not like to get:
For all your clothes and wedding-ring
    I've little doubt you fret.
My fair-haired son, my shame, my pride,
    Cling closer, closer yet:
Your sire would give broad lands for one
    To wear his coronet.

from THE PRINCE'S PROGRESS

. . . Too late for love, too late for joy,
    Too late, too late!
You loitered on the road too long,
    You trifled at the gate:
The enchanted dove upon her branch
    Died without a mate;
The enchanted princess in her tower
    Slept, died, behind the grate;
Her heart was starving all this while
    You made it wait.

'Ten years ago, five years ago,
    One year ago,
Even then you had arrived in time,
    Though somewhat slow;
Then you had known her living face
    Which now you cannot know:
The frozen fountain would have leaped,
    The buds gone on to blow,
The warm south wind would have awaked
    To melt the snow.

'Is she fair now as she lies?
    Once she was fair;
Meet queen for any kingly king,
    With gold-dust on her hair.
Now these are poppies in her locks,
    White poppies she must wear;
Must wear a veil to shroud her face
    And the want graven there:
Or is the hunger fed at length,
    Cast off the care?

'We never saw her with a smile
    Or with a frown;
Her bed seemed never soft to her
    Though tossed of down;
She little heeded what she wore,
    Kirtle, or wreath, or gown;
We think her white brows often ached
    Beneath her crown,
Till silvery hairs showed in her locks
    That used to be so brown.

'We never heard her speak in haste;
    Her tones were sweet,

And modulated just so much
    As it was meet:
Her heart sat silent through the noise
    And concourse of the street.
There was no hurry in her hands,
    No hurry in her feet;
There was no bliss drew nigh to her,
    That she might run to greet.

'You should have wept her yesterday,
    Wasting upon her bed:
But wherefore should you weep to-day
    That she is dead?
Lo we who love weep not to-day,
    But crown her royal head.
Let be these poppies that we strew,
    Your roses are too red:
Let be these poppies, not for you
    Cut down and spread.'

SISTER MAUDE

Who told my mother of my shame,
    Who told my father of my dear?
Oh who but Maude, my sister Maude,
    Who lurked to spy and peer.

Cold he lies, as cold as stone,
    With his clotted curls about his face:
The comeliest corpse in all the world
    And worthy of a queen's embrace.

You might have spared his soul, sister,
    Have spared my soul, your own soul too:

Though I had not been born at all,
    He'd never have looked at you.

My father may sleep in Paradise,
    My mother at Heaven-gate:
But sister Maude shall get no sleep
    Either early or late.

My father may wear a golden gown,
    My mother a crown may win;
If my dear and I knocked at Heaven-gate
    Perhaps they'd let us in:
But sister Maude, O sister Maude,
    Bide *you* with death and sin.

'NO, THANK YOU, JOHN'

I never said I loved you, John;
    Why will you tease me day by day,
And wax a weariness to think upon
    With always 'do' and 'pray'?

You know I never loved you, John;
    No fault of mine made me your toast:
Why will you haunt me with a face as wan
    As shows an hour-old ghost?

I dare say Meg or Moll would take
    Pity upon you, if you'd ask:
And pray don't remain single for my sake
    Who can't perform that task.

I have no heart?—Perhaps I have not;
    But then you're mad to take offence

That I don't give you what I have not got:
    Use your own common sense.

Let bygones be bygones:
    Don't call me false, who owed not to be true:
I'd rather answer 'No' to fifty Johns
    Than answer 'Yes' to you.

Let's mar our pleasant days no more,
    Song-birds of passage, days of youth:
Catch at to-day, forget the days before;
    I'll wink at your untruth.

Let us strike hands as hearty friends;
    No more, no less; and friendship's good:
Only don't keep in view ulterior ends,
    And points not understood

In open treaty. Rise above
    Quibbles and shuffling off and on.
Here's friendship for you if you like; but love,—
    No, thank you, John.

MIRAGE

The hope I dreamed of was a dream,
    Was but a dream; and now I wake,
Exceeding comfortless, and worn, and old,
    For a dream's sake.

I hang my harp upon a tree,
    A weeping willow in a lake;
I hang my silenced harp there, wrung and snapt
    For a dream's sake.

Lie still, lie still, my breaking heart;
  My silent heart, lie still and break:
Life, and the world, and mine own self are changed
  For a dream's sake.

THE LAMBS OF GRASMERE (1860)

The upland flocks grew starved and thinned:
  Their shepherds scarce could feed the lambs
Whose milkless mothers butted them,
  Or who were orphaned of their dams.
The lambs athirst for mother's milk
  Filled all the place with piteous sounds:
Their mothers' bones made white for miles
  The pastureless wet pasture grounds.

Day after day, night after night,
  From lamb to lamb the shepherds went,
With teapots for the bleating mouths,
  Instead of nature's nourishment.
The little shivering gaping things
  Soon knew the step that brought them aid,
And fondled the protecting hand,
  And rubbed it with a woolly head.

Then as the days waxed on to weeks,
  It was a pretty sight to see
These lambs with frisky heads and tails
  Skipping and leaping on the lea,
Bleating in tender trustful tones,
  Resting on rocky crag or mound,
And following the beloved feet
  That once had sought for them and found.

These very shepherds of their flocks,
  These loving lambs so meek to please,
Are worthy of recording words
  And honour in their due degrees:
So I might live a hundred years,
  And roam from strand to foreign strand,
Yet not forget this flooded spring
  And scarce-saved lambs of Westmoreland.

WIFE TO HUSBAND

Pardon the faults in me,
    For the love of years ago:
      Good-bye.
I must drift across the sea,
    I must sink into the snow,
      I must die.

You can bask in this sun,
    You can drink wine, and eat:
      Good-bye.
I must gird myself and run,
    Though with unready feet:
      I must die.

Blank sea to sail upon,
    Cold bed to sleep in:
      Good-bye.
While you clasp, I must be gone
    For all your weeping:
      I must die.

A kiss for one friend,
    And a word for two,—
      Good-bye:—
A lock that you must send,

A kindness you must do:
  I must die.

Not a word for you,
  Not a lock or kiss,
    Good-bye.
We, one, must part in two;
  Verily death is this:
    I must die.

PROMISES LIKE PIE-CRUST

Promise me no promises,
  So will I not promise you:
Keep we both our liberties,
  Never false and never true:
Let us hold the die uncast,
  Free to come as free to go:
For I cannot know your past,
  And of mine what can you know?

You, so warm, may once have been
  Warmer towards another one:
I, so cold, may once have seen
  Sunlight, once have felt the sun:
Who shall show us if it was
  Thus indeed in time of old?
Fades the image from the glass,
  And the fortune is not told.

If you promised, you might grieve
  For lost liberty again:
If I promised, I believe
  I should fret to break the chain.
Let us be the friends we were,

111

Nothing more but nothing less:
Many thrive on frugal fare
Who would perish of excess.

THE LOWEST PLACE

Give me the lowest place; not that I dare
   Ask for that lowest place, but Thou hast died
That I might live and share
   Thy glory by Thy side.

Give me the lowest place: or if for me
   That lowest place too high, make one more low
Where I may sit and see
   My God and love Thee so.

SONG

Two doves upon the selfsame branch,
   Two lilies on a single stem,
Two butterflies upon one flower:—
   Oh happy they who look on them!

Who look upon them hand in hand
   Flushed in the rosy summer light;
Who look upon them hand in hand,
   And never give a thought to night.

THE QUEEN OF HEARTS

How comes it, Flora, that, whenever we
Play cards together, you invariably,
   However the pack parts,
   Still hold the Queen of Hearts?

I've scanned you with a scrutinizing gaze,
Resolved to father these your secret ways:

But sift them as I will,
Your ways are secret still.

I cut and shuffle; shuffle, cut, again;
But all my cutting, shuffling, proves in vain:
    Vain hope, vain forethought too;
    That Queen still falls to you.

I dropped her once, prepense; but, ere the deal
Was dealt, your instinct seemed her loss to feel:
    'There should be one card more,'
    You said, and searched the floor.

I cheated once; I made a private notch
In Heart-Queen's back, and kept a lynx-eyed watch;
    Yet such another back
    Deceived me in the pack:

The Queen of Clubs assumed by arts unknown
An imitative dint that seemed my own;
    This notch, not of my doing,
    Misled me to my ruin.

It baffles me to puzzle out the clue,
Which must be skill, or craft, or luck in you:
    Unless, indeed, it be
    Natural affinity.

A DUMB FRIEND

I planted a young tree when I was young:
But now the tree is grown and I am old:
There wintry robin shelters from the cold
    And tunes his silver tongue.

113

A green and living tree I planted it,
A glossy-foliaged tree of evergreen:
All through the noontide heat it spread a screen
    Whereunder I might sit.

But now I only watch it where it towers:
I, sitting at my window, watch it tost
By rattling gale or silvered by the frost;
    Or, when sweet summer flowers,

Wagging its round green head with stately grace
In tender winds that kiss it and go by.
It shows a green full age: and what show I?
    A faded wrinkled face.

So often have I watched it, till mine eyes
Have filled with tears and I have ceased to see,
That now it seems a very friend to me,
    In all my secrets wise.

A faithful pleasant friend, who year by year
Grew with my growth and strengthened with my strength,
But whose green lifetime shows a longer length:
    When I shall not sit here

It still will bud in spring, and shed rare leaves
In autumn, and in summer-heat give shade,
And warmth in winter: when my bed is made
    In shade the cypress weaves.

LIFE AND DEATH

Life is not sweet. One day it will be sweet
    To shut our eyes and die;

114

Nor feel the wild flowers blow, nor birds dart by
    With flitting butterfly,
Nor grass grow long above our heads and feet,
Nor hear the happy lark that soars sky-high,
Nor sigh that spring is fleet and summer fleet,
    Nor mark the waxing wheat,
Nor know who sits in our accustomed seat.

Life is not good. One day it will be good
    To die, then live again;
To sleep meanwhile; so, not to feel the wane
    Of shrunk leaves dropping in the wood,
Nor hear the foamy lashing of the main,
Nor mark the blackened bean-fields, nor, where stood
    Rich ranks of golden grain,
Only dead refuse stubble clothe the plain:
    Asleep from risk, asleep from pain.

SOMEWHERE OR OTHER

Somewhere or other there must surely be
    The face not seen, the voice not heard,
The heart that not yet—never yet—ah me!
    Made answer to my word.

Somewhere or other, may be near or far;
    Past land and sea, clean out of sight;
Beyond the wandering moon, beyond the star
    That tracks her night by night.

Somewhere or other, may be far or near;
    With just a wall, a hedge, between;
With just the last leaves of the dying year
    Fallen on a turf grown green.

WEARY IN WELL-DOING

I would have gone; God bade me stay:
   I would have worked; God bade me rest.
He broke my will from day to day;
   He read my yearnings unexprest,
      And said them nay.

Now I would stay; God bids me go:
   Now I would rest; God bids me work.
He breaks my heart tost to and fro;
   My soul is wrung with doubts that lurk
      And vex it so.

I go, Lord, where Thou sendest me;
   Day after day I plod and moil:
But, Christ my God, when will it be
   That I may let alone my toil
      And rest with Thee?

SUMMER

Winter is cold-hearted,
   Spring is yea and nay,
Autumn is a weathercock
   Blown every way.
Summer days for me
When every leaf is on its tree;

When Robin's not a beggar,
   And Jenny Wren's a bride,
And larks hang singing, singing, singing,
   Over the wheat-fields wide,

And anchored lilies ride,
And the pendulum spider
Swings from side to side.

And blue-black beetles transact business,
    And gnats fly in a host,
And furry caterpillars hasten
    That no time be lost,
    And moths grow fat and thrive,
    And ladybirds arrive.

    Before green apples blush,
    Before green nuts embrown,
    Why one day in the country
    Is worth a month in town;
    Is worth a day and a year
Of the dusty, musty, lag-last fashion
    That days drone elsewhere.

WHAT WOULD I GIVE!

What would I give for a heart of flesh to warm me through,
Instead of this heart of stone ice-cold whatever I do!
Hard and cold and small, of all hearts the worst of all.

What would I give for words, if only words would come!
But now in its misery my spirit has fallen dumb.
O merry friends, go your way, I have never a word to say.

What would I give for tears! not smiles but scalding tears,
To wash the black mark clean, and to thaw the frost of years,
To wash the stain ingrain, and to make me clean again.

117

GROWN AND FLOWN

I loved my love from green of Spring
    Until sere Autumn's fall;
But now that leaves are withering
    How should one love at all?
    One heart's too small
For hunger, cold, love, everything.

I loved my love on sunny days
    Until late Summer's wane;
But now that frost begins to glaze
    How should one love again?
    Nay, love and pain
Walk wide apart in diverse ways.

I loved my love—alas to see
    That this should be, alas!
I thought that this could scarcely be,
    Yet has it come to pass:
    Sweet sweet love was,
Now bitter bitter grown to me.

EVE

'While I sit at the door,
Sick to gaze within,
Mine eye weepeth sore
For sorrow and sin:
As a tree my sin stands
To darken all lands;
Death is the fruit it bore.

118

'How have Eden bowers grown
Without Adam to bend them?
How have Eden flowers blown,
Squandering their sweet breath,
Without me to tend them?
The Tree of Life was ours,
Tree twelvefold-fruited,
Most lofty tree that flowers,
Most deeply rooted:
I chose the Tree of Death.

'Hadst thou but said me nay,
    Adam my brother,
I might have pined away—
    I, but none other:
God might have let thee stay
Safe in our garden,
By putting me away
Beyond all pardon.

'I, Eve, sad mother
Of all who must live,
I, not another,
Plucked bitterest fruit to give
My friend, husband, lover.
O wanton eyes, run over!
Who but I should grieve?
Cain hath slain his brother:
Of all who must die mother,
Miserable Eve!'

Thus she sat weeping,
Thus Eve our mother,
Where one lay sleeping

Slain by his brother.
Greatest and least
Each piteous beast
To hear her voice
Forgot his joys
And set aside his feast.

The mouse paused in his walk
And dropped his wheaten stalk;
Grave cattle wagged their heads
In rumination;
The eagle gave a cry
From his cloud station:
Larks on thyme beds
Forbore to mount or sing;
Bees drooped upon the wing;
The raven perched on high
Forgot his ration;
The conies in their rock,
A feeble nation,
Quaked sympathetical;
The mocking-bird left off to mock;
Huge camels knelt as if
In deprecation;
The kind hart's tears were falling;
Chattered the wistful stork;
Dove-voices with a dying fall
Cooed desolation,
Answering grief by grief.

Only the serpent in the dust,
Wriggling and crawling,
Grinned an evil grin and thrust
His tongue out with its fork.

SHALL I FORGET?

Shall I forget on this side of the grave?
I promise nothing: you must wait and see,
    Patient and brave.
(O my soul, watch with him, and he with me.)

Shall I forget in peace of Paradise?
I promise nothing: follow, friend, and see,
    Faithful and wise.
(O my soul, lead the way he walks with me.)

DEAD HOPE

Hope newborn one pleasant morn
    Died at even:
Hope dead lives nevermore,
    No not in heaven.

If his shroud were but a cloud
    To weep itself away—
Or were he buried underground
    To sprout some day!
But dead and gone is dead and gone,
    Vainly wept upon.

Nought we place above his face
    To mark the spot,
But it shows a barren place
    In our lot.

Hope has birth no more on earth
    Morn or even;
Hope dead lives nevermore,
    No not in heaven.

ENRICA

She came among us from the South,
    And made the North her home awhile;
    Our dimness brightened in her smile,
Our tongue grew sweeter in her mouth.

We chilled beside her liberal glow,
    She dwarfed us by her ampler scale,
    Her full-blown blossom made us pale—
She Summer-like and we like snow.

We Englishwomen, trim, correct,
    All minted in the selfsame mould,
    Warm-hearted but of semblance cold,
All-courteous out of self-respect.

She, woman in her natural grace,
    Less trammelled she by lore of school,
    Courteous by nature not by rule,
Warm-hearted and of cordial face.

So for awhile she made her home
    Among us in the rigid North,
    She who from Italy came forth
And scaled the Alps and crossed the foam.

But, if she found us like our sea,
    Of aspect colourless and chill,
    Rock-girt,—like all she found us still
Deep at our deepest, strong and free.

ITALIA, IO TI SALUTO

To come back from the sweet South, to the North
　　Where I was born, bred, look to die;
Come back to do my day's work in its day,
　　　Play out my play—
　　Amen, amen, say I.

To see no more the country half my own,
　　Nor hear the half familiar speech,
Amen, I say; I turn to that bleak North
　　　Whence I came forth—
　　The South lies out of reach.

But when our swallows fly back to the South,
　　To the sweet South, to the sweet South,
The tears may come again into my eyes
　　　On the old wise,
　　And the sweet name to my mouth.

A DAUGHTER OF EVE

　　A fool I was to sleep at noon,
　　　And wake when night is chilly
　　Beneath the comfortless cold moon;
　　A fool to pluck my rose too soon,
　　　A fool to snap my lily.

　　My garden-plot I have not kept;
　　　Faded and all-forsaken,
　　I weep as I have never wept:
　　Oh it was summer when I slept,
　　　It's winter now I waken.

123

Talk what you please of future Spring
     And sun-warmed sweet to-morrow:—
Stripped bare of hope and everything,
No more to laugh, no more to sing,
     I sit alone with sorrow.

A DIRGE

Why were you born when the snow was falling?
You should have come to the cuckoo's calling,
Or when grapes are green in the cluster,
Or at least when lithe swallows muster
   For their far off flying
   From summer dying.

Why did you die when the lambs were cropping?
You should have died at the apples' dropping,
When the grasshopper comes to trouble,
And the wheat-fields are sodden stubble,
   And all winds go sighing
   For sweet things dying.

'TO-DAY FOR ME'

     She sitteth still who used to dance,
She weepeth sore and more and more:—
Let us sit with thee weeping sore,
          O fair France.

     She trembleth as the days advance
Who used to be so light of heart:—
We in thy trembling bear a part,
          Sister France.

Her eyes shine tearful as they glance:
'Who shall give back my slaughtered sons?
'Bind up,' she saith, 'my wounded ones.'—
    Alas, France!

She struggles in a deathly trance,
As in a dream her pulses stir,
She hears the nations calling her,
    'France, France, France!'

Thou people of the lifted lance,
Forbear her tears, forbear her blood;
Roll back, roll back, thy whelming flood,
    Back from France.

Eye not her loveliness askance,
Forge not for her a galling chain:
Leave her at peace to bloom again,
    Vine-clad France.

A time there is for change and chance,
A time for passing of the cup:
And one abides can yet bind up
    Broken France.

A time there is for change and chance:
Who next shall drink the trembling cup,
Wring out its dregs and suck them up
    After France?

A CHRISTMAS CAROL

In the bleak mid-winter
    Frosty wind made moan,
Earth stood hard as iron,

Water like a stone;
Snow had fallen, snow on snow,
    Snow on snow,
In the bleak mid-winter
    Long ago.

Our God, Heaven cannot hold Him
    Nor earth sustain;
Heaven and earth shall flee away
    When he comes to reign:
In the bleak mid-winter
    A stable-place sufficed
The Lord God Almighty
    Jesus Christ.

Enough for Him, whom cherubim
    Worship night and day,
A breastful of milk
    And a mangerful of hay;
Enough for Him, whom angels
    Fall down before,
The ox and ass and camel
    Which adore.

Angels and archangels
    May have gathered there,
Cherubim and seraphim
    Thronged the air;
But only His mother
    In her maiden bliss
Worshipped the Beloved
    With a kiss.

What can I give Him.
    Poor as I am?

If I were a shepherd
   I would bring a lamb,
If I were a Wise Man
   I would do my part,—
Yet what I can I give Him,
   Give my heart.

YET A LITTLE WHILE

I dreamed and did not seek: to-day I seek
   Who can no longer dream;
But now am all behindhand, waxen weak,
   And dazed amid so many things that gleam
   Yet are not what they seem.

I dreamed and did not work: to-day I work,
   Kept wide awake by care
And loss, and perils dimly guessed to lurk;
   I work and reap not, while my life goes bare
   And void in wintry air.

I hope indeed; but hope itself is fear
   Viewed on the sunny side;
I hope and disregard the world that's here,
   The prizes drawn, the sweet things that betide;
   I hope, and I abide.

'I WISH I COULD REMEMBER'

'Era già l'ora che volge il desio.'—Dante
'Ricorro al tempo ch' io vi vidi prima.'—Petrarca

I wish I could remember that first day,
   First hour, first moment of your meeting me,

127

If bright or dim the season, it might be
Summer or Winter for aught I can say;
So unrecorded did it slip away,
    So blind was I to see and to foresee,
    So dull to mark the budding of my tree
That would not blossom yet for many a May.
If only I could recollect it, such
    A day of days! I let it come and go
    As traceless as a thaw of bygone snow;
It seemed to mean so little, meant so much;
If only now I could recall that touch,
    First touch of hand in hand—Did one but know!

'YOUTH GONE, AND BEAUTY GONE'

'E la Sua Volontade è nostra pace.'—Dante
Sol con questi pensier, con altre chiome.'—Petrarca

Youth gone, and beauty gone if ever there
    Dwelt beauty in so poor a face as this;
    Youth gone and beauty, what remains of bliss?
I will not bind fresh roses in my hair,
To shame a cheek at best but little fair,—
    Leave youth his roses, who can bear a thorn,—
I will not seek for blossoms anywhere,
    Except such common flowers as blow with corn.
Youth gone and beauty gone, what doth remain?
    The longing of a heart pent up forlorn,
        A silent heart whose silence loves and longs;
        The silence of a heart which sang its songs
    While youth and beauty made a summer morn,
Silence of love that cannot sing again.

128

THE KEY-NOTE

Where are the songs I used to know,
   Where are the notes I used to sing?
   I have forgotten everything
I used to know so long ago;
Summer has followed after Spring;
   Now Autumn is so shrunk and sere
I scarcely think a sadder thing
   Can be the Winter of my year.

Yet Robin sings through Winter's rest,
   When bushes put their berries on;
   While they their ruddy jewels don,
He sings out of a ruddy breast;
The hips and haws and ruddy breast
   Make one spot warm where snowflakes lie;
They break and cheer the unlovely rest
   Of Winter's pause—and why not I?

HE AND SHE

   'Should one of us remember,
     And one of us forget,
   I wish I knew what each will do,
     But who can tell as yet?'

   'Should one of us remember,
     And one of us forget,
   I promise you what I will do—
   And I'm content to wait for you,
     And not be sure as yet.'

A LIFE'S PARALLELS

Never on this side of the grave again,
    On this side of the river,
On this side of the garner of the grain,
    Never.

Ever while time flows on and on and on,
    That narrow noiseless river,
Ever while corn bows heavy-headed, wan,
    Ever.

Never despairing, often fainting, rueing,
    But look back, ah never!
Faint yet pursuing, faint yet still pursuing
    Ever.

PASTIME

A boat amid the ripples, drifting, rocking;
Two idle people, without pause or aim;
While in the ominous West there gathers darkness
    Flushed with flame.

A hay-cock in a hay-field, backing, lapping;
Two drowsy people pillowed round-about;
While in the ominous West across the darkness
    Flame leaps out.

Better a wrecked life than a life so aimless,
Better a wrecked life than a life so soft:
The ominous West glooms thundering, with its fire
    Lit aloft.

ONE SEA-SIDE GRAVE

Unmindful of the roses,
  Unmindful of the thorn,
A reaper tired reposes
  Among his gathered corn:
  So might I, till the morn!

Cold as the cold Decembers,
  Past as the days that set,
While only one remembers
  And all the rest forget,—
  But one remembers yet.

'BURY HOPE . . .'

Bury Hope out of sight,
  No book for it and no bell;
It never could bear the light
  Even while growing and well:
Think if now it could bear
The light on its face of care
And grey scattered hair.

No grave for Hope in the earth,
  But deep in that silent soul
Which rang no bell for its birth
  And rings no funeral toll.
Cover its once bright head;
Nor odours nor tears be shed:
It lived once, it is dead.

Brief was the day of its power,
  The day of its grace how brief:

131

As the fading of a flower,
    As the falling of a leaf,
So brief its day and its hour;
No bud more and no bower
Or hint of a flower.

Shall many wail it? not so:
    Shall one bewail it? not one:
Thus it hath been from long ago,
    Thus it shall be beneath the sun.
O fleet sun, make haste to flee;
O rivers, fill up the sea;
O Death, set the dying free.

The sun nor loiters nor speeds,
    The rivers run as they ran,
Thro' clouds or thro' windy reeds
    All run as when all began.
Only Death turns at our cries:—
Lo the Hope we buried with sighs
Alive in Death's eyes!

'ROSES ON A BRIER . . .'

Roses on a brier,
    Pearls from out the bitter sea,
Such is earth's desire
    However pure it be.

Neither bud nor brier,
    Neither pearl nor brine for me:
Be stilled, my long desire;
    There shall be no more sea.

Be stilled, my passionate heart;
   Old earth shall end, new earth shall be:
Be still, and earn thy part
   Where shall be no more sea.

'HEAVEN'S CHIMES ARE SLOW . . .'

Heaven's chimes are slow, but sure to strike at last:
   Earth's sands are slow, but surely dropping thro':
   And much we have to suffer, much to do,
     Before the time be past.

Chimes that keep time are neither slow nor fast:
   Not many are the numbered sands nor few:
   A time to suffer, and a time to do,
     And then the time is past.

'A COLD WIND STIRS . . .'

A cold wind stirs the blackthorn
   To burgeon and to blow,
Besprinkling half-green hedges
   With flakes and sprays of snow.

Thro' coldness and thro' keenness,
   Dear hearts, take comfort so:
Somewhere or other doubtless
   These make the blackthorn blow.

'LORD, WHAT HAVE I TO OFFER? . . .'

Lord, what have I to offer? Sickening fear
   And a heart-breaking loss.
Are these the cross Thou givest me? then dear
   I will account this cross.

If this is all I have, accept even this
   Poor priceless offering,
A quaking heart with all that therein is,
   O Thou my thorn-crowned King.

Accept the whole, my God, accept my heart
   And its own love within:
Wilt Thou accept us and not sift apart?
   —Only sift out my sin.

'THE FIELDS ARE WHITE . . .'

'The fields are white to harvest, look and see,
Are white abundantly.
The full-orbed harvest moon shines clear,
The harvest time draws near,
Be of good cheer.'

'Ah woe is me!
I have no heart for harvest time,
Grown sick with hope deferred from chime to chime!'

'But Christ can give thee heart Who loveth thee:
Can set thee in the eternal ecstasy
Of His great jubilee:
Can give thee dancing heart and shining face,

134

And lips filled full of grace,
And pleasures as the rivers and the sea.
Who knocketh at His door
He welcomes evermore:
Kneel down before
That ever-open door
(The time is short) and smite
Thy breast, and pray with all thy might.'

'What shall I say?'
                    'Nay, pray.
Tho' one but say "Thy will be done,"
He hath not lost his day
At set of sun.'

'MARGARET HAS A MILKING-PAIL'

Margaret has a milking-pail,
  And she rises early;
Thomas has a threshing-flail,
    And he's up betimes.
Sometimes crossing through the grass
  Where the dew lies pearly,
They say 'Good-morrow' as they pass
    By the leafy limes.

MAUDE

A Story for Girls

I

'A penny for your thoughts,' said Mrs Foster one bright July morning as she entered the sitting-room with a bunch of roses in her hand, and an open letter: 'A penny for your thoughts,' said she, addressing her daughter, who, surrounded by a chaos of stationery, was slipping out of sight some scrawled paper. This observation remaining unanswered, the mother, only too much accustomed to inattention, continued: 'Here is a not from your Aunt Letty; she wants us to go and pass a few days with them. You know Tuesday is Mary's birthday, so they mean to have some young people and cannot dispense with your company.'

'Do you think of going?' said Maude at last, having locked her writing-book.

'Yes, dear: even a short stay in the country may do you good, you have looked so pale lately. Don't you feel quite well? Tell me.'

'Oh yes; there is not much the matter, only I am tired and have a headache. Indeed, there is nothing at all the matter; besides, the country may work wonders.'

Half-satisfied, half-uneasy, Mrs Foster asked a few more questions, to have them all answered in the same style; vain questions, put to one who, without telling lies, was determined not to tell the truth.

When once more alone, Maude resumed the occupations which her mother's entrance had interrupted. Her writing-book was neither commonplace-book, album, scrap-book, nor diary; it was a compound of all these, and contained original compositions not intended for the public eye, pet extracts, extraordinary little sketches, and occasional tracts of journal. This choice collection she now proceeded to enrich with the following sonnet:—

Yes, I too could face death and never shrink:
But it is harder to bear hated life;
To strive with hands and knees weary of strife;
    To drag the heavy chains whose every link
    Galls to the bone; to stand upon the brink

Of the deep grave, nor drowse, though it be rife
With sleep; to hold with steady hand the knife
   Nor strike home: this is courage as I think.
Surely to suffer is more than to do:
   To do is quickly done; to suffer is
   Longer and fuller of heart-sicknesses:
   Each day's experience testifies of this:
Good deeds are many, but good lives are few;
   Thousands taste the full cup; who drains the lees?

having done which she yawned, leaned back in her chair, and wondered how she should fill up the time till dinner.

Maude Foster was just fifteen. Small though not positively short, she might easily be overlooked but would not easily be forgotten. Her figure was slight and well-made, but appeared almost high-shouldered through a habitual shrugging stoop. Her features were regular and pleasing, as a child she had been very pretty; and might have continued so but for a fixed paleness, and an expression, not exactly of pain, but languid and preoccupied to a painful degree. Yet even now, if at any time she became thoroughly aroused and interested, her sleepy eyes would light up with wonderful brilliancy, her cheeks glow with warm colour, her manner become animated, and drawing herself up to her full height she would look more beautiful than ever she did as a child. So Mrs Foster said, and so unhappily Maude knew. She also knew that people thought her clever, and that her little copies of verses were handed about and admired. Touching these same verses, it was the amazement of everyone what could make her poetry so broken-hearted as was mostly the case. Some pronounced that she wrote very foolishly about things she could not possibly understand; some wondered if she really had any secret source of uneasiness; while some simply set her down as affected. Perhaps there was a degree of truth in all these opinions. But I have said enough; the following pages will enable my readers to form their own estimate of Maude's character.

Meanwhile let me transport them to another sitting-room; but this time it will be in the country with a delightful garden look-out.

Mary Clifton was arranging her mother's special nosegay when that lady entered.

'Here, my dear, I will finish doing the flowers. It is time for you to go to meet your aunt and cousin; indeed, if you do not make haste, you will be too late.'

'Thank you, mamma; the flowers are nearly done;' and Mary ran out of the toom.

Before long she and her sister were hurrying beneath a burning sun towards the railway station. Through having delayed their start to the very last moment, neither had found time to lay hands on a parasol; but this was little heeded by two healthy girls, full of life and spirits, and longing, moreover, to spy out their friends. Mary wanted one day of fifteen; Agnes was almost a year older: both were well-grown and well-made, with fair hair, blue eyes, and fresh complexions. So far they were alike: what differences existed in other respects remain to be seen.

'How do you do, aunt? How do you do, Maude?' cried Mary, making a sudden dart forward as she discovered our friends, who, having left the station, had already made some progress along the dusty road. Then relinquishing her aunt to Agnes, she seized upon her cousin, and was soon deep in the description of all the pleasures planned for the auspicious morrow.

'We are to do what we like in the morning: I mean, nothing particular is arranged; so I shall initiate you into all the mysteries of the place; all the cats, dogs, rabbits, pigeons, etc.; above all, I must introduce you to a pig, a special *protégé* of mine: that is, if you are inclined, for you look wretchedly pale; aren't you well, dear?'

'Oh yes, quite well, and you must show me everything. But what are we to do afterwards?'

'Oh! afterwards we are to be intensely grand. All our young friends are coming, and we are to play at round games (you were always clever at round games), and I expect to have great fun. Besides, I have stipulated for unlimited strawberries and cream; also sundry tarts are in course of preparation. By the way, I count on your introducing some new game among us benighted rustics; you who come from dissipated London.'

138

'I fear I know nothing new, but will do my best. At any rate, I can preside at your toilet, and assist in making you irresistible.'

Mary coloured and laughed; then thought no more of the pretty speech, which sounded as if carefully prepared by her polite cousin. The two made a strong contrast: one was occupied by a thousand shifting thoughts of herself, her friends, her plans, what she must do, and what she would do; the other, whatever might employ her tongue, and to a certain extent her mind, had always an undercurrent of thought intent upon herself.

Arrived at the house, greetings were duly and cordially performed; also an introduction to a new and very fat baby, who received Maude's advances with a howl of intense dismay. The first day of a visit is often no very lively affair: so perhaps all parties heard the clock announce bed-time without much regret.

II

The young people were assembled in Mary's room, deep in the mysteries of the toilet.

'Here is your wreath, Maude; you must wear it for my sake, and forgive a surreptitious sprig of bay which I have introduced,' said Agnes, adjusting the last white rose, and looking affectionately at her sister and cousin.

Maude was arranging Mary's long fair hair with good-natured anxiety to display it to the utmost advantage.

'One more spray of fuchsia; I was always sure fuchsia would make a beautiful head-dress. There, now you are perfection; only look; look Agnes. Oh, I beg your pardon; thank you; my wreath is very nice, only I have not earned the bay.' She still did not remove it; and when placed on her dark hair it well became the really intellectual character of her face. Her dress was entirely white; simple, fresh, and elegant. Neither she nor Agnes would wear ornaments, but left them to Mary, in whose honour the entertainment was given, and who in all other respects was arrayed like her sister.

In the drawing-room Mary proceeded to set in order the presents received that morning—a handsomely bound Bible from her father, and a small prayer-book with cross and clasp from her mother; a bracelet of Maude's hair from her aunt; a cornelian heart from Agnes; and a pocket *bonbonnière* from her cousin, besides pretty trifles from her little brothers. In the midst of arrangements and re-arrangements the servant entered with a large bunch of lilies from the village school-children and the announcement that Mr and Mrs Savage were just arrived with their six daughters.

Gradually the guests assembled; young and old, pretty and plain; all alike seemingly bent on enjoying themselves; some with gifts, and all with cordial greetings for Mary, for she was a general favourite. There was slim Rosanna Hunt, her scarf arranged with artful negligence to hide a slight protrusion of one shoulder; and sweet Magdalen Ellis, habited as usual in quiet colours. Then came Jane and Alice Deverell, twins so much alike that few besides their parents knew them apart with any certainty; and their fair brother Alexis, who, had he been a girl, would have increased the confusion. There was little Ellen Potter, with a round rosy face like an apple, looking as natural and good-humoured as if, instead of a grand French governess, she had had her own parents with her like most of the other children; and then came three rather haughty-looking Miss Stantons, and pale Hannah Lindley the orphan; and Harriet Eyre, a thought too showy in her dress.

Mary, all life and spirits, hastened to introduce the new-comers to Maude; who, perfectly unembarrassed, bowed and uttered little speeches with the manner of a practical woman of the world; while the genuine, unobtrusive courtesy of Agnes did more towards making their guests comfortable than the eager good nature of her sister, or the correct breeding of her cousin.

At length the preliminaries were all accomplished, every one having found a seat, or being otherwise satisfactorily disposed of. The elders of the party were grouped here and there, talking and looking on; the very small children were accommodated in the adjoining apartment with a gigantic Noah's Ark: and the rest of the young people being at liberty to amuse themselves as fancy might prompt, a general appeal was made to Miss Foster for some game, novel, entertaining, and ingenious; or, some of the more diffident hinted, easy.

'I really know nothing new,' said Maude; 'you must have played at "Proverbs", "What's my thought like", "How do you like it", and "Magic music":—or stay, there is one thing we can try—*"Bouts-rimés"*.'

'What?' asked Mary.

' *"Bouts-rimés"*: it is very easy. Some one gives rhymes— mamma can do that—and then all of us fill them up as we think fit. A sonnet is the best form to select; but, if you wish, we could try eight, or even four lines.'

'But I am certain I could not make a couplet,' said Mary, laughing. 'Of course you would get on capitally, and Agnes might manage very well, and Magdalen can do anything; but it is quite beyond me: do pray think of something more suitable to my capacity.'

'Indeed I have nothing else to propose. This is very much better than mere common games; but if you will not try it, that ends the matter'; and Maude leaned back in her chair.

'I hope—' began Mary; but Agnes interposed:

'Suppose some of us attempt *"Bouts-rimés"*; and you meanwhile can settle what we shall do afterwards. Who is ready to test her poetic powers?—What, no one? Oh, Magdalen, pray join Maude and me.'

This proposal met with universal approbation, and the three girls retreated to a side-table, Mary, who supplied the rhymes, exacting a promise that only one sonnet should be composed. Before the next game was fixed upon, the three following productions were submitted for judgment to the discerning public. The first was by Agnes:

> Would that I were a turnip white,
> Or raven black,
> Or miserable hack
>> Dragging a cab from left to right;
>> Or would I were the showman of a sight,
> Or weary donkey with a laden back,
> Or racer in a sack,
>> Or freezing traveller on an Alpine height;

141

Or would I were straw-catching as I drown,
    (A wretched landsman I who cannot swim),
Or watching a lone vessel sink,
    Rather than writing; I would change my pink
Gauze for a hideous yellow satin gown,
    With deep-cut scolloped edges and a rim.

'Indeed, I had no idea of the sacrifice you were making,' observed Maude. 'You did it with such heroic equanimity. Might I, however, venture to hint that my sympathy with your sorrows would have been greater had they been expressed in metre.'

'There's gratitude for you,' cried Agnes gaily; 'what have you to expect, Magdalen?' and she went on to read her friend's sonnet:

    I fancy the good fairies dressed in white,
Glancing like moon-beams through the shadows black;
Without much work to do for king or hack.
    Training perhaps some twisted branch aright;
    Or sweeping faded Autumn leaves from sight
To foster embryo life; or binding back
Stray tendrils; or in ample bean-pod sack
    Bringing wild honey from the rocky height;
Or fishing for a fly lest it should drown;
    Or teaching water-lily heads to swim,
Fearful that sudden rain might make them sink;
    Or dyeing the pale rose a warmer pink;
Or wrapping lilies in their leafy gown,
    Yet letting the white peep beyond the rim.

'Well, Maude?'

'Well, Agnes; Miss Ellis is too kind to feel gratified at hearing that her verses make me tremble for my own: but such as they are, listen:

    Some ladies dress in muslin full and white,
Some gentlemen in cloth succinct and black;
Some patronise a dog-cart, some a hack,
    Some think a painted clarence only right.
    Youth is not always such a pleasing sight:
Witness a man with tassels on his back;

Or woman in a great-coat like a sack
  Towering above her sex with horrid height.
If all the world were water fit to drown
    There are some whom you would not teach to swim;
    Rather enjoying if you saw them sink;
  Certain old ladies dressed in girlish pink,
With roses and geraniums on their gown:
    Go to the Bason, poke them o'er the rim.'

'What a very odd sonnet,' said Mary after a slight pause; 'but surely men don't wear tassels.'

Her cousin smiled. 'You must allow for poetical licence; and I have literally seen a man in Regent Street wearing a sort of hooded cloak with one tassel. Of course everyone will understand the Bason to mean the one in St James' Park.'

'With these explanations your sonnet is comprehensible,' said Mary; and Magdalen added with unaffected pleasure: 'And without them it was by far the best of the three.'

Maude now exerted herself to amuse the party; and soon proved that ability was not lacking. Game after game was proposed and played at; and her fun seemed inexhaustible, for nothing was thought too nonsensical or too noisy for the occasion. Her good humour and animation were infectious: Miss Stanton incurred forfeits with the blandest smile; Hannah Lindley blushed and dimpled as she had not done for many months, Rosanna never perceived the derangement of her scarf; little Ellen exulted in freedom from school-room trammels; the twins guessed each other's thoughts with marvellous facility; Magdalen laughed aloud; and even Harriet Eyre's dress looked scarcely too gay for such an entertainment. Well was it for Mrs Clifton that the strawberries, cream, and tarts had been supplied with no niggard hand: and very meagre was the remnant left when the party broke up at a late hour.

III

Agnes and Mary were discussing the pleasures of the preceding evening as they sat over the unusually late breakfast, when Maude joined them. Salutations being exchanged and refreshments supplied to the last comer, the conversation was renewed.

'Who did you think was the prettiest girl in the room last night? our charming selves, of course, excepted,' asked Mary; 'Agnes and I cannot agree on this point.'

'Yes,' said her sister; 'we quite agree as to mere prettiness; only I maintain that Magdalen is infinitely more attractive than half the handsome people one sees. There is so much sense in her face and such sweetness. Besides, her eyes are really beautiful.'

'Miss Ellis has a characteristic countenance; but she appeared to me very far from the belle of the evening. Rosanna Hunt has much more regular features.'

'Surely you don't think Rosanna prettier than Jane and Alice,' interrupted Mary; 'I suppose I never look at those two without fresh pleasure.'

'They have good fair complexions, eyes, and hair, certainly,' and Maude glanced rather pointedly at her unconscious cousin; 'but to me they have a wax-dollish air which is quite unpleasant. I think one of the handsomest faces in the room was Miss Stanton's.'

'But she has such a disagreeable expression,' rejoined Mary hastily: then colouring, she half-turned towards her sister, who looked grave, but did not speak.

A pause ensued; and then Agnes said, 'I remember how prejudiced I felt against Miss Stanton when first she came to live here, for her appearance and manners are certainly unattractive: and how ashamed of myself I was when we heard that last year, through all the bitterly cold weather, she rose at six, though she never has a fire in her room, that she might have time before breakfast to make clothes for some of the poorest people in the village. And in the spring, when the scarlet fever was about, her mother would not let her go near the sick children for fear of contagion; so she saved up all her pocket money to buy wine and soup and such things for them as they recovered.'

'I dare say she is very good,' said Maude; 'but that does not make her pleasing. Besides, the whole family have that disagreeable expression, and I suppose they are not all paragons. But you have both finished breakfast, and make me ashamed by your diligence. What is that beautiful piece of work?'

The sisters looked delighted: 'I am so glad you like it, dear Maude. Mary and I are embroidering a cover for the lectern in our church; but we feared you might think the ground dull.'

'Not at all; I prefer those quiet shades. Why, how well you do it: is it not very difficult? Let me see if I understand the devices. There is the Cross and the Crown of Thorns; and those must be the keys of St Peter, with, of course, the sword of St Paul. Do the flowers mean anything?'

'I am the Rose of Sharon and the Lily of the Valley,' answered Agnes, pointing. 'That is the Balm of Gilead—at least, it is what we will call so; there are myrrh and hyssop, and that is a palm-branch. The border is to be vine-leaves and grapes; with fig-leaves at the corners, thanks to Mary's suggestions. Would you like to help us? There is plenty of room at the frame.'

'No; I should not do it well enough, and have no time to learn, as we go home to-morrow. How I envy you,' she continued in a low voice, as if speaking rather to herself than to her hearers: 'you who live in the country, and are exactly what you appear, and never wish for what you do not possess. I am sick of display, and poetry, and acting.'

'You do not act,' replied Agnes, warmly. 'I never knew a more sincere person. One difference between us is that you are less healthy and far more clever than I am. And this reminds me: Miss Savage begged me to ask you for some verses to put in her album. Would you be so very obliging? Any that you have by you would do.'

'She can have the sonnet I wrote last night.'

Agnes hesitated: 'I could not well offer her that, because—'

'Why? she does not "tower". Oh! I suppose she has some reprehensible old lady in her family, and so might feel hurt at my lynch-law.'

PART SECOND

I

Rather more than a year had elapsed since Maude parted from her cousins; and now she was expecting their arrival in London every minute: for Mrs Clifton, unable to leave her young family, had gratefully availed herself of Mrs Foster's offer to receive Agnes and Mary during the early winter months, that they might take music and dancing lessons with their cousin.

At length the rumbling of an approaching cab was heard; then a loud knock and ring. Maude started up: but instead of running out to meet her guests, began poking vigorously at the fire, which soon sent a warm, cheerful light through the apartment, enabling her, when they entered, to discern that Agnes had a more womanly air than at their last meeting, that Mary had out-grown her sister, and that both were remarkably good-looking.

'First let me show you your room; and then we can settle comfortably to tea; we are not to wait for mamma. She thought you would not mind sleeping together, as our house is so small; and I have done my best to arrange things for your taste, for I know of old how you have only one taste between you. Look, my room is next yours, so we can help each other very cosily: only pray don't think of unpacking now; there will be plenty of time this evening, and you must be famished: come.'

But Agnes lingered still, eager to thank her cousin for the good-natured forethought which had robbed her own apartment of flower-vases and inkstand for the accommodation of her guests. The calls of Mary's appetite were however imperious; and very soon the sisters were snugly settled on a sofa by the fire, while Maude, in a neighbouring arm-chair, made tea.

'How long it seems since my birthday party,' said Mary, as soon as the eatables had in some measure restored her social powers. 'Why, Maude, you are grown quite a woman; but you look more delicate than ever, and very thin: do you still write verses?' Then without waiting for a reply: 'Those which you gave Miss Savage for her album were very much admired; and Magdalen Ellis wished at the time for an autograph copy, only she had not courage to trouble you. But perhaps you are not aware that poor Magdalen has done with albums and such like, at least for the present: she has entered on her noviciate in the Sisterhood of Mercy established near our house.'

'Why poor?' said Maude. 'I think she is very happy.'

146

'Surely you would not like such a life,' rejoined her cousin. 'They have not proper clothes on their beds, and never go out without a thick veil, which must half-blind them. All day long they are at prayers, or teaching children, or attending the sick, or making things for the poor, or something. Is that to your taste?'

Maude half-sighed; and then answered: 'You cannot imagine me either fit or inclined for such a life; still I can perceive that those who are so are very happy. When I was preparing for confirmation, Mr Paulson offered me a district; but I did not like the trouble, and mamma thought me too unwell to be regular. I have regretted it since, though: yet I don't fancy I ever could have talked to the poor people or have done the slightest good. Yes, I continue to write now and then as the humour seizes me; and if Miss Ellis—'

'Sister Magdalen,' whispered Agnes.

'If Sister Magdalen will accept it, I will try and find her something admissible even within convent walls. But let us change the subject. On Thursday we are engaged to tea at Mrs Strawdy's. There will be no sort of party, so we need not dress or take any trouble.'

'Will my Aunt go with us?' asked Agnes.

'No. Poor mamma has been ailing for some time, and is by no means strong; so, as Mrs Strawdy is an old schoolfellow of hers, and a most estimable person, she thinks herself justified in consigning you to my guardianship. On Saturday we must go shopping, as Aunt Letty says you are to get your winter things in London; and I can get mine at the same time. On Sunday—or does either of you dislike Cathedral services?'

Agnes declared they were her delight; and Mary, who had never attended any, expressed great pleasure at the prospect of hearing what her sister preferred to all secular music.

'Very well,' continued Maude: 'we will go to St Andrew's then, and you shall be introduced to a perfect service; or, at any rate, to perhaps the nearest English approach to vocal perfection. But you know you are to be quite at home here; so we have not arranged any particular plans of amusement, but mean to treat you like ourselves. And now it is high time for you to retire.'

147

II

When Thursday arrived Agnes and Mary were indisposed with colds; so Mrs Foster insisted that her daughter should make their excuses to Mrs Strawdy. In a dismal frame of mind, Maude, assisted by her sympathising cousins, performed her slight preliminary toilet.

'You have no notion of the utter dreariness of this kind of invitation. I counted on your helping me through the evening, and now you fail me. Thank you, Mary; I shall not waste *eau de Cologne* on my handkerchief. Good-night both: mind you go to bed early, and get up quite well to-morrow. Good-night.'

The weather was foggy and raw as Maude stepped into the street; and proved anything but soothing to a temper already fretted; so by the time she had arrived at her destination, removed her walking things, saluted her hostess, and apologised for her cousins, her countenance had assumed an expression neither pleased nor pleasing.

'Let me present my nieces to you, my dear,' said Mrs Strawdy, taking her young friend by the hand and leading her towards the fire: 'This is Miss Mowbray, or, as you must call her, Annie; that is Caroline, and that Sophy. They have heard so much of you, that any further introduction is needless'; here Maude bowed rather stiffly: 'but as you are early people, you will excuse our commencing with tea, after which we shall have leisure for amusement.'

There was nothing so genuinely kind and simple as Mrs Strawdy's manner, that even Maude felt mollified, and resolved on doing her best not only towards suppressing all appearance of yawns, but also towards bearing her part in the conversation.

'My cousins will regret their indisposition more than ever, when they learn of how much pleasure it has deprived them,' said she, civilly addressing Miss Mowbray.

A polite bend, smile, and murmur formed the sole response. and once more a subject had to be started.

'Have you been very gay lately? I begin to acquire the reputation of an invalid; and so my privacy is respected.'

Annie coloured and looked excessively embarrassed; at last

she answered in a low hesitating voice: 'We go out extremely little, partly because we never dance.'

'Nor I either; it really is too fatiguing: yet a ball-room is no bad place for a mere spectator. Perhaps, though, you prefer the Theatre?'

'We never go to the play,' rejoined Miss Mowbray, looking more and more uncomfortable.

Maude ran on: 'Oh, I beg your pardon, you do not approve of such entertainments. I never go, but only for want of someone to take me.' Then addressing Mrs Strawdy: 'I think you know my aunt, Mrs Clifton?'

'I visited her years ago with your mamma,' was the answer: 'when you were quite a little child. I hope she continues in good health. Pray remember me to her and to Mr Clifton when you write.'

'With pleasure. She has a large family now, eight children.'

'That is indeed a large family,' rejoined Mrs Strawdy, intent meanwhile on dissecting a cake with mathematical precision: 'you must try a piece, it is Sophy's own manufacture.'

Despairing of success in this quarter, Maude now directed her attention to Caroline, whose voice she had not heard once in the course of the evening.

'I hope you will favour us with some music after tea; in fact, I can take no denial. You look too blooming to plead a cold, and I feel certain you will not refuse to indulge my love for sweet sounds: of your ability to do so I have heard elsewhere.'

'I shall be most happy; only you must favour us in return.'

'I will do my best,' answered Maude, somewhat encouraged; 'but my own performances are very poor. Are you fond of German songs? they form my chief resource.'

'Yes, I like them much.'

Baffled in this quarter also, Miss Foster wanted courage to attack Sophy, whose countenance promised more cake than conversation. The meal seemed endless: she fidgeted under the table with her fingers; pushed about a stool on the noiselessly-soft carpet until it came in contact with someone's foot; and at last fairly deprived Caroline of her third cup of coffee, by opening the piano and claiming the fulfilment of her promise.

The young lady complied with obliging readiness. She sang some simple airs, mostly religious, not indeed with much expression, but in a voice clear and warbling as a bird's. Maude felt consoled for all the contrarieties of the day; and was bargaining for one more song before taking Caroline's place at the instrument, when the door opened to admit Mrs and Miss Savage; who having only just reached town, and hearing from Mrs Foster that her daughter was at the house of a mutual friend, resolved on begging the hospitality of Mrs Strawdy, and renewing their acquaintance.

Poor Maude's misfortunes now came thick and fast. Seated between Miss Savage and Sophia Mowbray, she was attacked on either hand with questions concerning her verses. In the first place, did she continue to write? Yes. A flood of ecstatic compliments followed this admission: she was so young, so much admired, and, poor thing, looked so delicate. It was quite affecting to think of her lying awake at night meditating those sweet verses—('I sleep like a top,' Maude put in, drily)—which so delighted her friends, and would so charm the public if only Miss Foster could be induced to publish. At last the bystanders were called upon to intercede for a recitation.

Maude coloured with displeasure; a hasty answer was rising to her lips, when the absurdity of her position flashed across her mind so forcibly that, almost unable to check a laugh in the midst of her annoyance, she put her handkerchief to her mouth. Miss Savage, impressed with a notion that her request was about to be complied with, raised her hand, imploring silence; and settled herself in a listening attitude.

'You will excuse me,' Maude at last said very coldly; 'I could not think of monopolising every one's attention. Indeed you are extremely good, but you must excuse me.' And here Mrs Savage interposed, desiring her daughter not to tease Miss Foster; and Mrs Strawdy seconded her friend's arguments by a hint that supper would make its appearance in a few minutes.

Finally the maid announced that Miss Foster was 'fetched'; and Maude, shortening her adieus and turning a deaf ear to

Annie's suggestions that their acquaintance should not terminate with the first meeting, returned home dissatisfied with her circumstances, her friends, and herself.

III

It was Christmas Eve. All day long Maude and her cousins were hard at work putting up holly and mistletoe in wreaths, festoons, or bunches, wherever the arrangement of the rooms admitted of such embellishment. The picture-frames were hidden behind foliage and bright berries; the bird-cages were stuck as full of green as though it had been Summer. A fine sprig of holly was set apart as a centre-bit for the pudding of next day: scratched hands and injured gowns were disregarded: hour after hour the noisy bustle raged: until Mrs Foster, hunted from place to place by her young relatives, heard, with inward satisfaction, that the decorations were completed.

After tea Mary set the backgammon board in array and challenged her aunt to their customary evening game: Maude, complaining of a headache, and promising either to wrap herself in a warm shawl or to go to bed, went to her room, and Agnes, listening to the rattle of the dice, at last came to the conclusion that her presence was not needed downstairs, and resolved to visit the upper regions. Thinking that her cousin was lying down tired and might have fallen asleep, she forbore knocking; but opened the door softly and peeped in.

Maude was seated at a table surrounded by the old chaos of stationery; before her lay the locking manuscript-book, into which she had just copied something. That day she had appeared more than usually animated: and now supporting her forehead upon her hand, her eyes cast down till the long lashes nearly rested upon her cheeks, she looked pale, languid, almost in pain. She did not move, but let her visitor come close to her without speaking. Agnes thought she was crying.

'Dear Maude, you have overtired yourself. Indeed, for all our sakes, you should be more careful': here Agnes passed her arm affectionately round her friend's neck: 'I hoped to find you fast asleep, and instead of this you have been writing in the cold.'

'You will stay to Communion to-morrow?' asked Maude after a short silence, and without replying to her cousin's remarks; even these few words seemed to cost her an effort.

'Of course I shall; why, it is Christmas Day: at least I trust to do so. Mary and I have been thinking how nice it will be for us all to receive together: so I want you to promise that you will pray for us at the Altar, as I shall for you. Will you?'

'I shall not receive to-morrow,' answered Maude; then hurrying on as if to prevent the other from remonstrating: 'No: at least I will not profane Holy Things; I will not add this to all the rest. I have gone over and over again, thinking I should come right in time, and I do not come right. I will go no more.'

Agnes turned quite pale: 'Stop,' she said, interrupting her cousin: 'stop; you cannot mean—you do not know what you are saying. You will go no more? Only think if the struggle is so hard now, what it will be when you reject all help.'

'I do not struggle.'

'You are ill to-night,' rejoined Agnes very gently; 'you are tired and over-excited. Take my advice, dear; say your prayers and get to bed. But do not be very long; if there is anything you miss and will tell me of, I will say it in your stead. Don't think me unfeeling: I was once on the very point of acting as you propose. I was perfectly wretched: harassed and discouraged on all sides. But then it struck me—you won't be angry?—that it was so ungrateful to follow my own fancies, instead of at least endeavouring to do God's Will: and so foolish too; for if our safety is not in obedience, where is it?'

Maude shook her head: 'Your case is different. Whatever your faults may be (not that I perceive any), you are trying to correct them; your own conscience tells you that. But I am not trying. No one will say that I cannot avoid putting myself forward and displaying my verses. Agnes, you must admit so much.'

Deep-rooted indeed was that vanity which made Maude take pleasure, on such an occasion, in proving the force of arguments directed against herself. Still Agnes would not yield; but resolutely did battle for the truth.

'If hitherto it has been so, let it be so no more. It is not

152

too late; besides, think for one moment what will be the end of this. We must all die: what if you keep to your resolution, and do as you have said, and receive the Blessed Sacrament no more?'—Her eyes filled with tears.

Maude's answer came in a subdued tone: 'I do not mean never to communicate again. You remember Mr Paulson told us last Sunday that sickness and suffering are sent for our correction. I suffer very much. Perhaps a time will come when these will have done their work on me also; when I shall be purified indeed and weaned from the world. Who knows? the lost have been found, the dead quickened.' She paused as if in thought; then continued: 'You partake of the Blessed Sacrament in peace, Agnes, for you are good; and Mary, for she is harmless: but your conduct cannot serve to direct mine, because I am neither the one nor the other. Some day I may be fit again to approach the Holy Altar, but till then I will at least refrain from dishonouring it.'

Agnes felt almost indignant. 'Maude, how can you talk so? this is not reverence. You cannot mean that for the present you will indulge vanity and display; that you will court admiration and applause; that you will take your fill of pleasure until sickness, or it may be death, strips you of temptation and sin together. Forgive me; I am sure you never meant this: yet what else does a deliberate resolution to put off doing right come to?—and if you are determined at once to do your best, why deprive yourself of the appointed means of grace? Dear Maude, think better of it'; and Agnes knelt beside her cousin, and laid her head against her bosom.

But still Maude, with a sort of desperate wilfulness, kept saying: 'It is of no use; I cannot go to-morrow; it is of no use.' She hid her face, leaning upon the table and weeping bitterly; while Agnes, almost discouraged, quitted the room.

Maude, once more alone, sat for some time just as her cousin left her. Gradually the thick, low sobs became more rare; she was beginning to feel sleepy. At last she roused herself with an effort, and commenced undressing; then it struck her that her prayers had still to be said. The idea of beginning them frightened her, yet she could not settle to sleep without saying something.

Strange prayers they must have been, offered with a divided heart and a reproachful conscience. Still they were said at length; and Maude lay down harassed, wretched, remorseful, everything but penitent. She was nearly asleep, nearly unconscious of her troubles, when the first stroke of midnight sounded.

PART THIRD
I
Agnes Clifton to Maude Foster

12th June 18—

My dear Maude,

Mamma has written to my aunt that Mary's marriage is fixed for the 4th of next month: but as I fear we cannot expect you both so many days before the time, I also write, hoping that you at least will come without delay. At any rate, I shall be at the station to-morrow afternoon with a chaise for your luggage, so pray take pity on my desolate condition, and avail yourself of the three o'clock train. As we are both bridesmaids elect, I thought it would be very nice for us to be dressed alike, so have procured double quantity of everything; thus you will perceive no pretence remains for your lingering in smoky London.

You will be amused when you see Mary: I have already lost my companion. Mr Herbert calls at least once a day, but sometimes oftener; so all day long Mary is on the alert. She takes much more interest in the roses over the porch than was formerly the case; the creepers outside the windows require continual training, not to say hourly care: I tell her the constitution of the garden must have become seriously weakened lately. One morning I caught her before the glass, trying the effect of syringa (the English orange-blossom, you know) in her hair. She looked such a darling. I hinted how flattered Mr Herbert would feel when I told him; which provoked her to offer a few remarks on old maids. Was it not a shame?

Last Thursday Magdalen Ellis was finally received into the Sisterhood of Mercy. I wished much to be present, but could not, as the whole affair was conducted quite privately; only her parents were admitted. However, I made interest for a lock of her beautiful hair, which I prize highly. It makes me sad to look at it; yet I know she has chosen well; and will, if she perseveres, receive hereafter an abundant recompense for all she has forgone here. Sometimes I think whether such a life can be suited to me; but then I could not leave mamma: indeed, that is just what Magdalen felt so much. I met her yesterday walking with some poor children. Her veil was down, nearly hiding her face; still I fancy she looked thoughtful, but very calm and happy. She says she always prays for me, and asked my prayers; so I begged her to remember you and Mary. Then she inquired how you are; desiring her kindest love to you, and assuring me she makes no doubt your name will be known at some future period: but checking herself almost immediately, she added that she could fancy you very different, as pale Sister Maude. This surprised me, I can fancy nothing of the sort. Then, having nearly reached my home, we parted.

What a document I have composed; I who have not one minute to spare from Mary's trousseau. Will you give my love to my aunt; and request her from me to permit your immediately coming to your affectionate cousin,

Agnes M. Clifton.

P.S.—Mary would doubtless send a message were she in the room; I conjecture her to be lurking about somewhere on the watch. Good-bye: or rather, Come.

—Maude handed the letter to her mother. 'Can you spare me, mamma? I should like to go, but not if it is to inconvenience you.'

'Certainly you shall go, my dear. It is a real pleasure to hear you express interest on some point, and you cannot be with anyone I approve of more than Agnes. But you must make haste with the packing now. I will come and help you in a few minutes.'

Still Maude lingered. 'Did you see about Magdalen? I wonder what made her think of me as a Sister. It is very nice of her; but then she is so good she never can conceive what I am like. Mamma, should you mind my being a nun?'

'Yes, my dear; it would make me miserable. But for the present take my advice and hurry a little, or the train will leave without you.'

Thus urged, Maude proceeded to bundle various miscellaneous goods into a trunk; the only article on the safety of which she bestowed much thought being the present destined for Mary: a sofa-pillow worked in glowing shades of wool and silk. This she wrapped carefully in cloth, and laid at the bottom: then over it all else was heaped without much ceremony. Many were the delays occasioned by things mislaid, which must be looked for, ill-secured, which must be re-arranged; or remembered too late, which yet could not be dispensed with, and so must be crammed in somewhere. At length, however, the tardy preparations were completed; and Maude, enveloped in two shawls, though it was the height of summer, stepped into a cab; promising strict conformity to her mother's injunction that both the windows should be kept closed.

Half-an-hour had not elapsed when another cab drove up to the door; and out of it Maude was lifted perfectly insensible. She had been overturned; and, though no limb was broken, had neither stirred nor spoken since the accident.

II
Maude Foster to Agnes Clifton

2nd July 18—

My dear Agnes,
You have heard of my mishap? it keeps me not bed-ridden, but sofa-ridden. My side is dreadfully hurt; I looked at it this morning for the first time, but hope never again to see so shocking a sight. The pain now and then is extreme; though not always so; sometimes, in fact, I am unconscious of any injury.

Will you convey my best love and wishes to Mary, and tell her how much I regret being away from her at such a time, especially as mamma will not hear of leaving me.

The surgeon comes twice a day to dress my wounds; still, all the burden of nursing falls on poor mamma. How I wish you were here to help us both; we should find plenty to say.

But, perhaps, ere many months are past I shall be up and about, when we may go together on a visit to Mary; a most delightful possibility. By the way, how I should love a baby of hers, and what a pretty little creature it ought to be. Do you think Mr Herbert handsome? hitherto I have only had a partial opinion.

Ugh, my side! it gives an awful twinge now and then. You need not read my letter; but I must write it, for I am unable to do anything else. Did the pillow reach safely? It gave me so much pleasure to work it for Mary, who, I hope, likes it. At all events, if not to her taste, she may console herself with the reflection that it is unique; for the pattern was my own designing.

Here comes dinner; good-bye. When will anything so welcome as your kind face gladden the eyes of your affectionate

Maude Foster?

P.S.—I have turned tippler lately on port wine three times a day. 'To keep you up,' says my doctor: while I obstinately refuse to be kept up, but insist on becoming weaker and weaker. Mind you write me a full history of your grand doings on a certain occasion: not omitting a detailed account of the lovely bride, her appearance, deportment, and toilet. Good-bye once more: when shall I see you all again?

III

Three weeks had passed away. A burning sun seemed baking the very dust in the streets, and sucking the last remnant of moisture from the straw spread in front of Mrs Foster's house, when the sound of a low muffled ring was heard in the sick-room and Maude, now entirely confined to her bed, raising herself on one arm, looked eagerly towards the door; which opened to admit a servant with the welcome announcement that Agnes had arrived.

After tea Mrs Foster, almost worn out with fatigue, went to bed, leaving her daughter under the care of their guest. The first greetings between the cousins had passed sadly enough. Agnes perceived at a glance that Maude was, as her last letter hinted, in a most alarming state; while the sick girl, well aware of her condition, received her friend with an emotion which showed she felt it might be for the last time. But soon her spirits rallied.

'I shall enjoy our evening together so much, Agnes,' said she, speaking now quite cheerfully. 'You must tell me all the news. Have you heard from Mary since your last despatch to me?'

'Mamma received a letter this morning before I set off; and she sent it, hoping to amuse you. Shall I read it aloud?'

'No; let me have it myself.' Her eye travelled rapidly down the well-filled pages, comprehending at a glance all the tale of happiness. Mr and Mrs Herbert were at Scarborough; they would thence proceed to the Lakes; and thence, most probably, homewards, though a prolonged tour was mentioned as just possible. But both plans seemed alike pleasing to Mary; for she was full of her husband, and both were equally connected with him.

Maude smiled as paragraph after paragraph enlarged on the same topic. At last she said: 'Agnes, if you could not be yourself, but must become one of us three: I don't mean as to goodness, of course, but merely as regards circumstances, would you change with Sister Magdalen, with Mary, or with me?'

'Not with Mary, certainly. Neither should I have courage to change with you; I never should bear pain so well: nor yet with Sister Magdalen; for I want her fervour of devotion. So at present I fear you must even put up with me as I am. Will that do?'

There was a pause. A fresh wind had sprung up, and the sun was setting.

At length Maude resumed: 'Do you recollect last Christmas Eve when I was so wretched, what shocking things I said? How I rejoice that my next Communion was not indeed delayed till sickness had stripped me of temptation and sin together.'

'Did I say that? It was very harsh.'

'Not harsh: it was just and right as far as it went; only something more was required. But I never told you what altered me. The truth is, for a time I avoided as much as possible frequenting our parish church, for fear of remarks. Mamma, knowing how I love St Andrew's, let me go there very often by myself, because the walk is too long for her. I wanted resolution to do right; yet, believe me, I was very miserable; how I could say my prayers at that period is a mystery. So matters went on; till one day as I was returning from a shop, I met Mr Paulson. He enquired immediately whether I had been staying in the country. Of course I answered, No. Had I been ill? again, No. Then gradually the whole story came out. I never shall forget the shame of my admissions; each word seemed forced from me, yet at last, all was told. I will not repeat all we said then, and on a subsequent occasion when he saw me at church: the end was, that I partook of the Holy Communion on Easter Day. That was indeed a Feast.'

Then changing the conversation abruptly, Maude said: 'Agnes, it would only pain mamma to look over everything if I die; will you examine my verses and destroy what I evidently never intended to be seen. They might all be thrown away together, only mamma is so fond of them. What will she do?'—and the poor girl hid her face in the pillows.

'But is there no hope, then?'

'Not the slightest, if you mean of recovery; and she does not know it. Don't go away when all's over, but do what you can to comfort her. I have been her misery from my birth till now; there is no time to do better, but you must leave me, please; for I feel completely exhausted. Or, stay one moment. I saw Mr Paulson again this morning, and he promised to come to-morrow to administer the Blessed Sacrament to me; so I count on you and mamma receiving with me, for the last time perhaps: will you?'

'Yes, dear Maude. But you are so young, don't give up hope. And now would you like me to remain here during the night? I can establish myself quite comfortably on your sofa.'

'Thank you, but it could only make me restless. Good-night, my own dear Agnes.'

'Good-night, dear Maude. I trust to rise early to-morrow, that I may be with you all the sooner.' So they parted.

That morrow never dawned for Maude Foster.

. . . . . .

Agnes proceeded to perform the task imposed upon her, with scrupulous anxiety to carry out her friend's wishes. The locked book she never opened; but had it placed in Maude's coffin, with all its words of folly, sin, vanity; and, she humbly trusted, of true penitence also. She next collected the scraps of paper found in her cousin's desk and portfolio, or lying loose upon the table; and proceeded to examine them. Many of these were mere fragments, many half-effaced pencil scrawls, some written on torn backs of letters, and some full of incomprehensible abbreviations.

159

Agnes was astonished at the variety of Maude's compositions. Piece after piece she committed to the flames, fearful lest any should be preserved not intended for general perusal: but it cost her a pang to do so; and to see how small a number remained for Mrs Foster. Of two only she took copies for herself.

The first was evidently composed subsequently to Maude's accident:

> Fade, tender lily,
>> Fade, O crimson rose,
> Fade every flower,
>> Sweetest flower that blows.
>
> Go, chilly Autumn,
>> Come, O Winter cold;
> Let the green stalks die away
>> Into common mould.
>
> Birth follows hard on death,
>> Life on withering.
> Hasten, we shall come the sooner
>> Back to pleasant Spring.

The other was a sonnet, dated the morning before her death:

> What is it Jesus saith unto the soul?
> 'Take up the Cross, and come, and follow Me.'
> This word He saith to all; no man may be
>> Without the Cross, wishing to win the goal.
>> Then take it bravely up, setting thy whole
> Body to bear; it will not weigh on thee
> Beyond thy utmost strength: take it; for He
>> Knoweth when thou art weak, and will control
> The powers of darkness that thou need'st not fear.
>> He will be with thee, helping, strengthening,
> Until it is enough: for lo, the day
> Cometh when He shall call thee: thou shalt hear
>> His Voice that says: 'Winter is past, and Spring
> Is come; arise, My Love, and come away.'

Agnes cut one long tress from Maude's head; and on her return home laid it in the same paper with the lock of Magdalen's hair. These she treasured greatly, and, gazing on them, would long and pray for the hastening of that eternal morning which shall reunite in God those who in Him, or for His sake, have parted here.

Amen for us all.

THE END